The Art and Craft of Chainsaw Carving

Chapel Publishing Co. Inc.

1970 Broad Street • East Petersburg, PA 17520 • www.carvingworld.com

Publisher: Alan Giagnocavo

Project Editor: Ayleen Stellhorn

Desktop Specialist: Linda L. Eberly, Eberly Designs Inc.

Interior Photography: Debra Y. Fichtner; Carl Shuman, Owl Hill Studios

Cover Photography: Carl Shuman, Owl Hill Studios

ISBN # 1-56523-128-7

Library of Congress Card Number: 00-110651

To order your copy of this book,
please send check or money order
for cover price plus $3.00 shipping to:
Fox Books
1970 Broad Street
East Petersburg, PA 17520

Manufactured in Korea

This book is dedicated to my secretary and best friend Debbie.

Debbie did all of the typing and much of the other work on this book. She runs the Timbercrafts office, the shop and my house.

Debbie is a native American artisan in her own right, doing jewelry, beadwork, basketry, wool spinning, chip carving and more. She is also a heavy equipment operator. Deb is somewhat of an herbalist and appears to have healing powers. She may possibly be a witch doctor. She has also been a model for many Native American paintings.

Deb did all of the action and in-progress photography for this book.

Table of

Acknowledgements vi
About the Author vii
Introduction viii

PART ONE - The Art of Chainsaw Carving 1

Hal MacIntosh 2
Terry Boquist 18
Scott Crocker 19
Scott Crocker and Terry Boquist 21
Don Etue 22
Steve Heller 24
Edwin K. LaFitte 27
A.J. Luter 29
Pat McVay 31
Dennis Roghair 34
Alexandre Safonov 39
Mark Tyoe 40

Northeastern Chainsaw Carving Championship **44**

Gary Patterson 44	Rolf Schmalzer 46	Dennis Beach 50, 51
Wayne Harvey, Sr 45	Robert Dieterle 46	Don Etue 51, 52
Frank Bono 45	Rich Anderson 47, 48	Duane Bender . . . 51, 52, 53
John Byrdson 45	Brent Butler 47	Mark Tyoe 54
Rick Pratt 45	Terry Boquist 47	Kim Kingrey 55
Ken Dudley 46	Elwood Woody Adams . 48, 49	Jeff Pinney 56
Christopher LaMontain . . 46	Ben Risney 49, 50	Rolf Schmalzer 56

Best Chainsaw Artist Shop Contest **57**

Brian McEneny 57	Joe Serres 60	Jim Clark 62
Don Etue 59	Jeff Laskowski 61	
John Wyell 59	Mark Tyoe 61	

Contents

PART TWO - The Basics of Chainsaw Carving

Saw Chain 63

Guide Bars 69

Drive Sprockets 70

Chainsaw Specifications Charts 73

Chainsaw Gallery 77

Carver/Carpenter Bar Specifications Chart 87

A Condensed History of the Chainsaw 89

PART THREE – Chainsaw Carving

Chainsaw Safety 93

Choosing a Team of Saws 95

Project Wood 96

How to 99

    Line Drawing 99

    Shallow Relief 101

    Pierced Relief 104

    Silhouette Relief 109

    Step Cutting – Craft-style Bear Head 110

    Step Cutting – Log Cabin with Trees 112

    Step Cutting – Life-size Sculpture 116

Life-size Heron 118

Totem Poles 132

PART FOUR – Chainsaw Patterns

Design Notes 135

Carving Humans 138

Acknowledgments

I wish to thank all of the people who made this book possible.

The following individuals, manufacturers and advertising managers have been kind enough to allow us to use their information herein to aid you, the reader, in a better understanding of chainsaw products. However, they are in no way responsible for anything I have chosen to include in this book. Their information is included merely to aid you in a safe, efficient endeavor.

Ken Morrison, editor of *Chainsaw Age Magazine* (now *Power Equipment Trade Magazine*) from 1979 to 1990—Ken supplied the information on G. B. Titanium Carving Bar Mounts. He owns Ken Morrison Marketing Service in Washington.

Jim Hampton, G.B. American.

Dan Shell, Managing Editor, *Power Equipment Trade Magazine,* a Hatton Brown Publication—Dan constructed and allows us to use the chainsaw specification charts.

Dave Tilton, Jr., of the Tilton Equipment Company—Dave supplied the work on Jonsered and Olympyk chainsaws. The Tilton Equipment Company imports Jonsered and Olympyk chain saws and sells safety equipment and parts for numerous other brands. The staff at Tilton Equipment has proved invaluable to me over the past dozen years in answering many of my saw-related questions.

Brian Lepine of the Carlton Saw Chain Company, Oregon—Brian constructed the most comprehensive technical data booklet of saw chains, bars and sprockets I have ever seen. Much of this booklet is reprinted herein. If there are any defects in the transfer of information to this manuscript, I assure you it is my fault and not that of Brian Lepine or the Carlton Saw Chain Company.

Erik Granberg, owner of Granberg International—Granberg manufactures the legendary Granberg Alaskan Mill, the Mini Mill and numerous related products.

Erin Cosgrove, Marketing Coordinator, Husqvarna Chain Saws—Erin provided the specifications sheet on Husqvarna chainsaws.

The editors also wish to thank Bill Bailey and Steve Erbach of Bailey's Inc. (P.O. Box 550, Laytonville, CA 95454, 800-322-4539, *www.baileys-online.com*) and artist Pat McVay (*www.mcvaysculpture.com*) for their invaluable insight.

About the Author

Hal MacIntosh's first book, *The Tree Climbers Guide Book,* was written, illustrated and sold in the early 1970s. He made his first chainsaw carving—a working goose decoy—in the mid-1960s at a moose and caribou camp in White Bear Lake, New Foundland. His first chainsaw carving book, *The Chain Saw Craft Book,* was in stores by January 1980. The Chain Saw Craft Book was written and illustrated at the Fish Creek Ranch in southwest Colorado and was sent to the publisher hand-printed. During the 1980s his "More Rewarding Wood Pile" series appeared in *Mother Earth News, Outdoor Life* and other outdoor magazines. Between 1989 and 1993, Hal produced the book and video series entitled, *Chain Saw Arts and Crafts Making and Marketing.* Twenty-some of his articles have appeared in *Chip Chats,* the magazine of the National Wood Carvers Association, in the past several years. *Chainsaw Carving: The Art and Craft* is Hal's latest publication.

Introduction

To choose the material for any how-to book or institutional text book, one must first decide on the degree of previous knowledge each user of the text will have. For a book such as this, it is impossible to know how much previous knowledge a reader is going to have—whether it be technical data pertaining to tools; anatomy of a given species; or general ability to draw, create or carve. Therefore, I will attempt to include something of value for every carver's possible weak points.

In this book you will notice that the photos of the same carving appear more than once. This is deliberate. A relief may be used to demonstrate the use of a chain-saw-milled slab, and in another section of the book, the same relief may be used to illustrate anatomical correctness, texturing, shop layout, design or any other of the numerous skills needed in chainsaw carving.

As I write this introduction and the table of contents for this now-completed work, I notice that I have covered only approximately half of what I originally intended to include. I have previously produced two other books and two videos of to hours each on chainsaw carving, and these missing subjects are not covered there either. I hope to cover these subjects in my next volume.

In closing, if you intend to be a safe, successful chainsaw carver, know and understand your chainsaw's cutting and safety systems. Be willing to study and research each subject you are going to carve. Do not use saws too small or too big for the job. Never use a saw too large or too fast for your strength or ability. Maintain your equipment to the manufacturer's specifications.

Hal MacIntosh

Part One: Chainsaw Art

Periodically, Timbercrafts runs a Best Chainsaw Artist Shop Contest. The contest rose out of the many pictures I receive each year from chainsaw artists across the country. The main reason for staging this contest is to explore the marketing questions that many of us have. The contest has led us to the following conclusions about how to best market yourself and your work.

• If a choice is available a carver should design and build his shop around the style of work he does and the type of customer he attracts.

• Among the things all successful shops have in common is that they keep their buyers and carvings dry, clean and safe. Customers who are entertained or inspired want to own a piece of your work.

• If you have to consider a daily cash flow as a means of survival, such as many other small businessmen do, then a diversification of styles, sizes, subject matter and price ranges is a necessity.

• Location and the laws, building codes, ordinances and the existing surrounding architecture and landscaping will also play a major role in shop design.

• Price and financing is probably the largest factor, unless you are a trust funder or have a rich spouse or won the lottery. I am not aware of any chainsaw carvers that fit in these categories, though luck and accidental timing are probably another factor.

• I know of three chainsaw carvers who have a PhD, but a lot more have a GED, neither of which are necessities for a successful chainsaw carver.

The very best chainsaw carver I know does little if anything to promote his work or himself. He relies mostly on his previous works being seen in public places and acquiring custom orders in the same manner. I also know carvers who have been working at this art for only two or three years and already earn more money than some who have been carving two or three decades. And then there's Gary Patterson who travels the country in a 33-foot-long by 8-foot-wide motor home towing a 16-foot-long trailer for his carvings. This year, his Eastern tour was packed with pre-scheduled show, competitions and sales, all of which add greatly to a yearly income.

After going over hundreds of marketing ideas and the pros and cons of each, one commonality appears. The same basic principles apply to improving marketing that apply to improving your carving. Each carver's drive, imagination, ambition, constant study and improvement lead toward a more successful future. You'll find pictures of shop entries and the winners on pages 57–62.

On the following pages, you'll find chainsaw carvings from some of the best chainsaw carvers around the country. Their work represents a wide variety of styles and techniques.

SAFETY FIRST

Some of the photos in Part One depict chainsaw carvers operating equipment outside of the recommended safety practices. These shots were taken candidly, without the benefit of a professional photographer or a fully equipped, environmentally controlled studio. Do not attempt to operate a chainsaw without proper safety equipment and a thorough knowledge of the saw's operation as based on the manufacturer's guidelines.

Hal MacIntosh—The author and his shop

The author and two of his old trucks. Both trucks have power tailgates. Your personal advertising on your delivery of show trucks extends your advertising and promoting capability, while you are away from the shop. It also adds a touch of professionalism when you arrive on a construction site to deliver or work on custom orders. It is also the best form of promotion you can do for your shop.

The author with two life-sized chainsaw carvings outside his shop.

Several views of the author's old shop.

The author's old shop. The two groupings of rapid production pieces above—quick sales inventory bears—shows the need for heavy production.

In order to maximize the full potential of a crotch in a tree, I set the bigger saws aside. Most of the work on this piece was accomplished with 50cc or 60cc saw fitted with a 12 in. or 14 in. sprocket nose utility bar. Black walnut is hard and may contain small pockets of decay. Therefore, the design had to be altered as I proceeded. No major step cuts should be made when working on a piece such as this.

Old Style generic bears, by Hal MacIntosh, 1989.

New and Old World Santas, by Hal MacIntosh, 1989.

Eight coons on flat back, 10 ft. 6 in. entrance way column, by Hal MacIntosh.

Raccoon and owl, by Hal MacIntosh.

Chainsaw carvings in Dunton Hot Springs, southwest Colorado, by Hal MacIntosh, 1983. Above: Pierced relief. Below: Ponderosa Pine Relief.

Burl bowl and stool, by Hal MacIntosh.

This fireman was carved by blocking out small sections at a time. Each section was carved down to the approximate form and size. The entire carving was roughed out in this manner. I used a fireman trophy as a model for this carving. To be sure of the detail on the coat buckles, hat and boots, I borrowed fire fighting clothing from a local fire company. The extended nozzle was added by drilling the center of both pieces to be fitted. I used a 14 in. length of 5/8 in. hardwood dowel to join the two pieces.

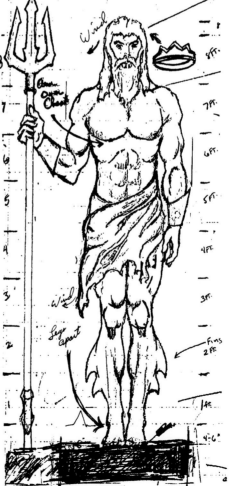

The drawing to the left is a customer's faxed sketch with alteration notations marked in. We used the eight-head scale for this Neptune rendering. Note that Neptune's hands appear too thick in the photo. This was corrected before the second oiling.

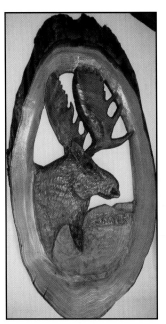

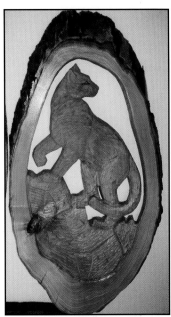

Pierced relief carvings, by Hal MacIntosh.

Benches by the author,
Durango, Colorado, 1981.

Rockie Mountain Juniper
Eastern Red Cedar
Ponderosa Pine

One Big-Hearted Clown

When my slate is full, I often connect people who want carvings with other chainsaw carvers—either to do an on-site carving, demonstrate at a show or provide inventory for a shop. Among the many requests I have received from people wanting to locate a chainsaw carver, the following request and consequent job in 1994 was easily the most rewarding.

The request from the advertising department of Homelite Textron was to locate a chainsaw carver willing to travel to Atlanta, Georgia, to the site of a new Ronald McDonald House. Once there, the carver would carve a 13-foot tall, 52-inch wide oak stump into a statue of Ronald McDonald.

I agreed to find someone. I made five or six phone calls, and for one reason or another, none of the carvers would commit to the commission. I had promised I would locate a carver. So, to keep that promise, I decided to do the job myself.

Considering the size of the log, the four days I had to complete the job, and the fact that it was tough old oak, I decided to do a 6-foot practice model in white pine at my shop in New York. I had one photo of Ronald and a small caricature statue that did not look like him at all. I tried to blend both into my carving.

After completing the practice carving, my secretary, Debbie, painted it. It wasn't bad for a first try, and it gave me the confidence I needed to tackle the oak stump.

Once in Atlanta, I found that the 13-foot oak stump had a cavity at the top, so four feet of the log had to be cut off. The carving, minus the base, is about $8^{1}/2$ feet tall. I started on May 18 and had almost finished on May 21 when a severe wind and rain storm blew up and tore down a lot of trees in Atlanta. Quite a few of those trees made the evening news that night, but the stump survived.

I finished the carving, but had to stay over until Monday for photo shoots and interviews with the media. That's when I got to meet the Man himself: Mr. Ronald McDonald. I donated the 6-ft. carving I had made at my shop to him.

Meeting Ronald and these other great people was worth the 1,020-mile trip. Everyone involved in the project—from the laborers who helped with the scaffold, up to the headman—were wonderful. All worked in unison beyond belief. The job turned out to be a richly rewarding experience, but leaving them with something was even better.

Ronald McDonald and the author clown around while checking out the thumbnail proportions. The carving of Ronald holding a miniature Ronald McDonald house is carved in oak and stands 8 ft. 6 in. tall.

As practice for the commission, the author carved a 6-ft.-tall statue of Ronald at my New York studio. Here, I am presenting the pine sculpture to the real Ronald McDonald as a gift.

The Runamuck Project

This private home sits on an 80-acre parcel in New York state. The frame work is heavy-duty steel. All of the steel is covered by structural wood, decorative wood and stone. An Early American, hand-hewn post-and-beam barn was reassembled as the living room.

My small part in this project, as defined by the project's designer, called for four 12 ft. column bear-themed pieces. The columns at the left front of the house represent the owner's four children in one tree and the two parents in the other. The columns featuring single bears at the pool porch are to assure the theme is carried throughout the project. I also carved a 30 ft. totem pole on the far side of the lake, visible from the pool. Small, red cedar bear carvings that I made were used in and on the railings.

I also provided loads of logs of various diameters, lengths and shapes. All of the logs had to be peeled and textured, some had to be chainsaw milled in half. I also provided some burls and knot swells for decorative and functional placement. A considerable number of hours were consumed by hollowing, notching and shaping logs for placement in the structure.

This hollow log has a 40 in. wide piece removed up to the 12 foot mark, which is the distance to the outer edge of the two steel columns we are covering. We slowly boom and slide the log near the deck in hopes of achieving an acceptable multi-angled notch on both sides of the log.

Another truck load of interior and exterior design logs is loaded at Timbercrafts for delivery to Runamuck. Debarking, skimming and texturing was done with a chainsaw.

The carvings above, along with another of two adult bears, is used as ornamental covers for 5 in. x 5 in. steel support columns. I found a 5 in. wide board, nailed it down and marked the carving with a heavy duty Magic Marker. Then I marked my bar for a 6 in. deep cut. I made the 6 in. deep cut with an upper mid-range saw fitted with a utility bar. I then changed to a detailing saw with a dime tip bar and a $1/4$ pitch saw chain to make a series of 6 in. deep cuts perpendicular to the two long cuts and two inches apart. I used a small one-handed sledge hammer to knock out most of the blocks. A flat bladed adz was used to clean up most of the remaining wood in the notch. Several times there were stubborn knots that had to be ground away with the tip of the saw bar.

Hal MacIntosh

The two bear columns at the front of the house are in place.

This hollow log is yellow poplar, also called tulip tree or tulip poplar. The butt cut is eight feet in diameter. The tree once stood on the Andrew Jackson estate in Nashville, Tennessee, but was blown over during a storm.

We removed a 40 in. wide piece of wood up to the 12-ft. mark. These are the measurements of the two steel columns we are covering. A door will be carved in the front of the log as an entranceway to the tree house.

The two exposed beam ends are carved into matching bear heads. These will be viewed from a distance, and the craft-style angles will stand out more vividly than the rounder, smoother lines of a more realistic rendering.

A ground level single adult bear and tree carving helps to support the log beam. Notice the two beams protruding from the roof near the chimney. These will be carved into bear heads.

The author notched and jointed the logs for the structure. He regularly uses 15 different methods of jointing logs, but this particular method is his favorite.

At press time, the project was almost complete. Only a few months of work are left on the house.

Catskill Corners

Catskill Corners is located in the Northern Catskill Mountains of upstate New York and is the home of the world's largest kaleidoscope. Dean Gitter is the owner and creator of the Kaleidoscope Complex, which includes the dynamically designed Spotted Dog Restaurant, named after the Fireman's mascot, the dalmation. Inside the barn style shopping mall are numerous stores and other eateries.

Across from the Kaleidoscope entrance is a store called Wild Things. On each side of the entranceway to this store are 10 ft. by 40 in. chainsaw carvings, with 20 percent of the back removed to fit them flatly against the wall. On the left are three bears in a tree; on the right are eight raccoons in a tree.

Outside the complex is an 11 ft. wood spirit face in a log and one of my personally created characters called a Catskillen. I incorporated Rip Van Winkle, a local character, the little guy that coaxed him to drink and my generic Hick all into one character.

At the east side of the complex is a park and memorial to John Burroughs, where my 1996 carving of him stands with the plaque fastened to a boulder.

To the west of this complex and separated by space and trees, is a sprawling log structure complex called, The Resort at Catskill Corners and the Catamount Cafe. The steel framed wooden sign is capped with oiled white pine logs, 20 to 23 ft. long, with recessed grooves 14 in. wide and 12 in. deep. On this part of the project I borrowed a friend's family heirloom adz to use in addition to my chainsaws and Log Wiz. I don't use many non-motorized tools, but the adz is sure a good one.

In the front of the Cafe, in the garden, is one of my large

A life-sized bear stands on a catalpa shelf over one of the complex's large fireplaces.

chainsaw carved Catalpa Mountain Lions.

Inside, over one of the large fire places is a catalpa burl shelf appearing to hold a bronze mountain lion, done by an artist unknown to me. There are other bronze cats and cat tapestries spread over the property. My chainsaw craft skills were also used to fit the new structure with the old and to cap over the edges of remodeled areas.

Dozens of carpenters, artists and heavy equipment operators worked together for the greatest efficiency, comfort and cost control under the direction of Ken Graham, Dean Gitter's right hand man. Ken knows every nail, board, log, wire used on all of these projects.

I have only done three other projects bigger than this one in the past several years. This one however, is my favorite. I assume the reason for this is the spirit of the buyer. Dean Gitter is a creative thinker and art buyer and does not care about what some people in the art world would call politically or socially correct. Dean just buys what appeals to him and custom orders the sculptures he feels appropriate for a particular location.

The three grooved log caps add to the aesthetics of the structure and hide the steel frame.

JOHN BURROUGHS
1837 – 1921
NATURALIST · CONSERVATIONIST · EDUCATOR

FROM HUMBLE BEGINNINGS IN THESE
CATSKILL MOUNTAINS, HE ROSE TO BE A
FRIEND OF THE POWERFUL AND FAMOUS,
A VOICE RESPECTED THROUGHOUT THE
LAND, A PROTECTOR OF ALL THINGS,
LARGE AND SMALL, THAT WE HERE
LOVE AND VALUE.

ARTIST: H. MACINTOSH, 1996

This carving of John Burroughs (left) was a custom order by the author. A plaque by the carving tells of Burroughs' life.

While chainsaw carving a pair of matching interior architectural enhancements for the Inn at Catskill Corners, I noticed a rifle muzzle loader ball in a chunk of wood that I had removed near the heart of the tree. I took the chunk of wood in my shop showroom and left it on the rear door entrance table.

Some weeks later, on a rainy day, I took the block of wood in my finishing room and was going to clean it up slightly, seal the ball in the wood and give it to Dean Gitter, the founder and creator of Catskill Corners. I was carefully carving the wood from the edges of the ball when it fell out. I saw a substantial amount of hair. I also noticed extreme flattening of the ball to indicate it was fired at close range or had an extreme charge of black powder behind it. I carefully pushed the ball back in its 200-plus year old resting place and sealed my find in a clear plastic bag.

Being somewhat excited about my find, I called the pathology department at Five Rivers Environmental Center in Delmar and spoke with Ward Stone, the head pathologist. He asked me to bring the ball in for his examination. His first study through a micro-scope found tis-sue, fiber, and several types of hair. Later, he told me that some of the hair appeared to be snout hair of a black bear.

At this writing, I am still not sure if the ball was shot through a bear's head or a human wearing fur clothing. The best dating I can come up with is that the rifle ball was fired into the bear and the tree around 1778. The tree was about 20 years old at that time.

The tree was removed on State Route 214 at the Creek Side Lodge, adjacent to Stony Creek, a few minutes from Phoneica, New York. Today, over 200 years later, black bears are still seen almost daily in this area (except during hibernation).

The Catskillen, by Hal MacIntosh

Wood Spirit, by Hal MacIntosh

Terry Boquist

Grandalf Wizard, 7 ft. yard light.

American Elm and Juniper Chair, 1996.

Redwood Burl Griffin Table, 1998.

Birds Eye Maple Chair, 1997.

Ships figurehead
(lifesize), 1996.

Elf, 4 ft., 1994.

Great Blue Heron,
5 ft., 1995.

Wolf Table, 1992.

Native Spirit, 10 ft., 1990.

Call of the Buffalo, 10 ft., 1990.

Richard the Lionheart, 7 ft., 1992.

Scott Crocker and Hobart Reitan—Camelot Bar, 1991.

Wolf Bed, 1996.

King Size Bed Frame, 1998.

Close-up of bed.

White Cedar and Juniper Dining Room
Table. Top by Scott Crocker; base by Terry Boquist.

Cedar and Juniper Bed,
7 ft., 1994.

Don Etue

International Nautical Chainsaw Carving Championship, West Port, Washington, August 1994. First Place People and Carver. 9 ft. x 4 ft.

The completed piece can be seen in front of a real estate office in Des Moines, Washington.

The Sea Captain. Western red cedar, 8 ft.

Spruce, International Nautical Chainsaw Carving Championship, West Port, Washington, 1997. First Place Judges Choice, 8 ft. x 3 ft.

Eagles in
Paradise.
Old growth
cedar,
6 ft. x 6 ft.

Logger.
Old growth cedar,
6 ft.

Dolphins.
Old growth
cedar, 8 ft.

This carving,
shown outside
Don's shop in
Ocean Shores,
Washington,
sold for $5,000.
1996.

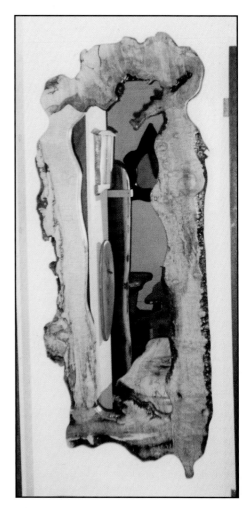

Country Western Band

Puppy Love

Man with a Large Belly

Pegasus Colt

A. J. Luter holds a bear carved in under 10 minutes.

Outdoor Classroom. A human hand releases a tiny "fry" which will grow to a giant salmon. Red cedar, 30 ft. long, 1998. Note the belted kingfisher on the left end of the log.

The back of the Outdoor Classroom log was used to show more of the life cycle of the salmon.

Ten-foot Orca whale carved from a 500-year-old Cedar root. 1989.

A close-up of the belted kingfisher.

Pat McVay is a full-time sculptor, working primarily on large wood projects. His other mediums include stone, clay, cast metals, concrete, ice and snow. He is a founding member of the Cascade Chainsaw Sculptors Guild (1986) and along with Jessie Groeschen, founded *The Cutting Edge,* newsletter of chainsaw sculpture. (*The Cutting Edge,* 8000 Scatchet Head Road, Clinton, WA 98236)

Sea Turtle, glass top table base. Red cedar, 6 ft. x 4 ft., 1994.

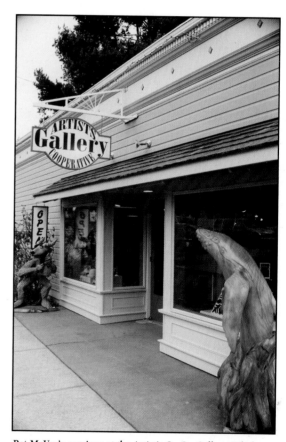

Pat McVay's carvings at the Artist's Co-Op Gallery. Whale Watching (right), Westport contest piece, Sitka spruce, 1997. Thief of Technology (left), pine.

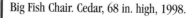

Big Fish Chair. Cedar, 68 in. high, 1998.

Dennis Roghair

Voyager. Carved from a 46,000-pound redwood log. This carving is located at River Side Park in Pine City, Minnesota. The man in the photographs is not the artist, but was included in the shot to show the scale of the carving.

Dennis Roghair

Dance with Dolphin, by Alexandre Safonov.

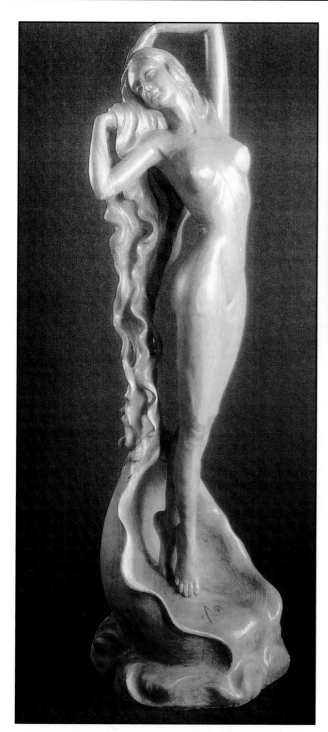

Birth of Venus, 7 ft. tall, cedar, by Alexandre Safonov.

Daughter of the Sea, 10 ft. tall, spruce, by Alexandre Safonov. Won first place at Westport, Washington, 1998.

Sacred Heart, 6 ft. tall, laminated basswood, by Alexandre Safonov. Commissioned by St. Andrew Catholic Church, Sumner, Washington.

by Mark Tyoe

Mark Tyoe

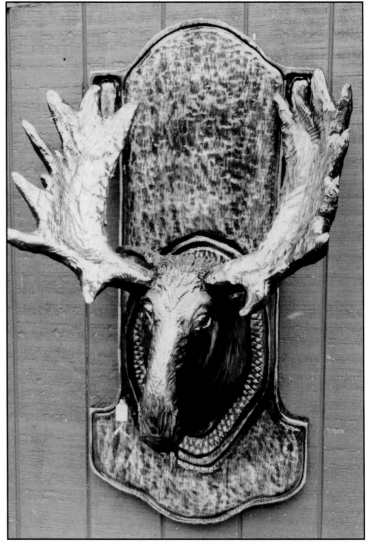

Northeastern Chainsaw Carving Championship
Tuper Lake, New York

Gary Patterson exhibits carvings at the Northeastern Chainsaw Carving Championship at Tuper Lake, New York. 1995–1996.

Wayne Harvey Sr. included 16 bears and 19 trees in this 1994 carving.

Frank Bono. 1994.

John Byrdson. 1994.

Rick Pratt. 1996.

Carving Championship

Christopher LaMontain. 1996.

Ken Dudley. 1997.

Rolf Schmalzer. 1996.

Robert Dieterle. 1997.

Brent Butler. 1998.

Rich Anderson. 1997.

Rich Anderson. 1994.

Rich Anderson. 1998.

Terry Boquist. 1997.

Rich Anderson. 1996.

Rich Anderson. 1996.

Elwood Woody Adams. 1997.

Elwood Woody Adams. 1998.

Elwood Woody Adams. 1997.

Ben Risney. 1996.

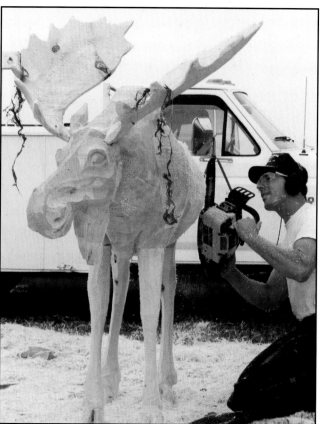

Carving Championship

Ben Risney. 1995.

Dennis Beach. 1994–1996.

Dennis Beach. 1994–1996.

Dennis Beach. 1994–1996.

Dennis Beach. 1994–1996.

Don
Etue.
1994.

Duane Bender. 1994.

Don Etue. 1994.

Duane Bender. 1994.

Duane Bender. 1996.

Duane Bender. 1996.

Duane Bender. 1995.

Mark Tyoe, 1996, Novice Winner.

Mark Tyoe

Mark Tyoe

Mark Tyoe

Kim Kingrey of Indiana, Quick Cut,
May 2000

Jeff Pinney of Pennsylvania, May 2000

Rolf Schmalzer of Massachusetts, May 2000

Best Chainsaw Artist Shop Contest

The winner of the 1996 Best Chainsaw Artist Shop Contest was Brian McEneny of Seal Rock, Oregon. His shop features a large parking lot, a well-thought-out floor plan and beautifully landscaped grounds.

The second story loft provides additional show room space and storage.

Brian's outside courtyard, with its wandering paths is breath-takingly beautiful, with outstanding wood sculptures of Pacific Coast wildlife spread out tastefully over the grounds.

The first floor of his shop is a 1,440 square foot showroom and a small shop.

Don Etue at his shop in Washington State.

Don Etue's shop is located in Ocean Shores, Washington.

Shop of John Wyell, Thurmont, Maryland.

The shop of the
"Carving Cowboy"
Joe Serres.
Winnetoon, Nebraska.

The shop and works of
Jeff Laskowski.
St. Francis, Wisconsin.

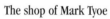

The shop of Mark Tyoe

The shop and carvings of
Jim Clark.
Manilla, Iowa.

Part Two:
Chainsaw Basics

A cut-away of a Jonsered saw shows the inner workings of a chainsaw.

Chain saws have changed. Older saws ran with chain speeds as slow as 600 feet per minute. There was enough raw power to allow the operator to almost ignore all of the chain maintenance problems. If a chain was misfiled, there was more than enough power to still make it cut. Chain speeds were so slow that bar and chain wear was not much of a problem. Also, the chains were physically larger (.404" and $1/2$" pitch, for example) and could handle the abuse.

Today's saws are not as forgiving. These smaller powerheads have less than half the engine displacement of the older saws and run much smaller chain (usually .325 and $3/8$" pitch) at speeds of up to 3,000 to 4,000 feet per minute. If saw chain is not maintained properly, modern chain saws will not perform well and the result will be chain or guide bar failures and operator frustration.

In this part of the book, I'll outline the specifics of chain saws—their different parts, how they work and how to maintain them. My goal in presenting this technical information is to give you a greater understanding of the chain saw, which will in turn make you a safer and more efficient chain saw carver.

SAW CHAIN

This section was compiled with the cooperation of the Carlton Saw Chain Company. The technical data was supplied by Carlton in hopes that all operator of chain saws may achieve safer, more productive and more economically efficient use of their saw chain, bars and sprockets.

Each manufacturer of saw chain has its own maintenance theories on its products. Check with your local authorized servicing dealer selling the brand of product you are using. This article contains several lines which pertain to Carlton Saw Chain only.

To help you properly maintain saw chain, avoid the problems of poor maintenance and recognize the wear patterns that can cause saw chain and guide bar failure, it is essential to first learn how saw chain cuts wood. You might be surprised to learn that a cutter tooth must actually leave the guide bar to cut wood efficiently.

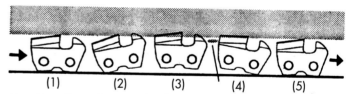

(1) (2) (3) (4) (5)
How Saw Chain Cuts Wood – The cutter tooth actually leaves the guide bar to bite into the wood and remove a wood chip.

All saw chain cuts with a rocking motion. When cutting properly, saw chain resembles a dolphin swimming in the ocean. As the cutter enters the wood, the "leading edge" starts to bite (1) causing the cutter to rock back as far as the depth gauge will allow (2). The cutter is now in the "attack position." The cutter jumps off the guide bar and into the wood (3). Chain tension and power from the saw pull the cutter back out of the wood and the severed chip exits from the underside of the cutter (4). The cutter then returns to its original position (5). Any condition that upsets this smooth and efficient rocking motion will have a

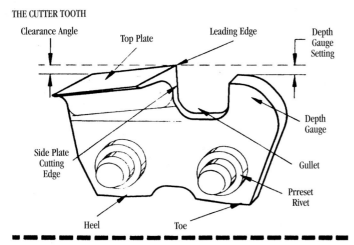

THE CUTTER TOOTH

Clearance Angle
Top Plate
Leading Edge
Depth Gauge Setting
Depth Gauge
Gullet
Side Plate Cutting Edge
Prreset Rivet
Heel
Toe

THE RIVET

Rivet Hubs
Flange Bearing

THE DRIVE LINK

Rivet Bearing Cage
Tang

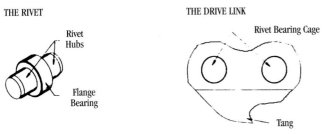

TIE STRAPS

Tie Strap
Preset Tie Strap

To help you understand saw chain, a brief review of the component parts is helpful. Please use the above illustration to reference the terms used in this section.

FILE SIZE APPLICATION CHART

CHAIN PITCH/TYPE	USE FILE SIZE
1/4", 1/8"	5/32"
3/8" Low Profile	5/32"
.325" Chisel & Semi-chisel	3/16"
Carlton .325" Chisel	11/64"
3/8" Chipper	7/32"
3/8" Chisel & Semi-chisel	7/32"
Carlton 3/8" Chisel	13/64"
.404" Chipper	7/32"
.404" Chisel & Semi-chisel	1/4"

negative effect on the life, performance and cutting efficiency of any saw chain.

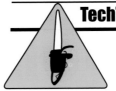

TechTip

Saw chain parts may look alike but they are not interchangeable. Never install used repair parts or mix different manufacturer's parts when repairing or making up chain loops. Always use only the manufacturer's replacement parts.

Saw Chain Components

Depth gauges are often called rakers because some think they "rake" out the severed chips, just like raking leaves. The actual function of the depth gauge is to determine how far the cutter will rock back in position and ultimately how large a bite the cutter will take. It is normal for the depth gauge to sink into the wood.

The "clearance angle" of the cutter in the cutter tooth illustration is the reason why saw chain is able to cut with an efficient rocking motion. As you can see, the rear of the top plate is lower in height than the front, which allows it to tip forward and exit the wood cleanly. Without a clearance angle, the cutter's top plate complicates the process of depth gauge maintenance.

The overall width of the cut that the saw chain makes in the wood is called kerf. Technically, kerf is determined by the outsides of the left hand and right hand cutters.

Saw Chain Kerf

Kerf

Left Hand Cutter
Right Hand Cutter

The word pitch actually means size. The larger the pitch (measured in thousandths of an inch) the larger the saw chain. Pitch is determined by measuring the distance between the centerlines of three consecutive rivets and dividing this distance in half. In other words, 3/8 pitch saw chain

Saw Chain Pitch

This distance divided by two

A1
A1

(.375") measures 3/4 of an inch (.750") between the centerlines.

Saw chain gauge refers to the thickness of the drive link tangs that fit into the guide bar groove and is also measured

Saw Chain Gauge

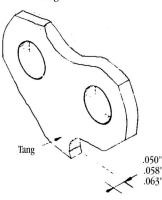

Tang

.050",
.058"
.063"

in thousandths of an inch. There are three standard gauges for hand-held chain saw cutting chain; .050", .058" and .063". It is important that the saw chain's gauge match the guide bar gauge.

My personal method for determining the gauge of an unmarked saw chain, brought into my shop, is to try it in a new known 50 gauge bar first, then a 58 gauge bar. I use a section of new saw chain placed in the bar groove to determine the width or gauge of the groove.

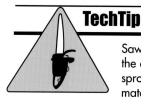

TechTip

Saw chain pitch must match the pitch of the drive sprocket and the guide bar sprocket tip. Saw chain gauge must match the gauge of the guide bar. Any mismatch on the items listed above will lead to premature failure of saw chain, guide bar or drive sprocket.

Cutter Designs

Tooth size, shape and "leading edge" determine the efficiency and durability of saw chain and provide a history lesson in saw chain design. Most of the saw's power is consumed by cutting the cross grains of the wood.

The first modern cutter design is called Chipper. It has a thick top plate and side plate as well as a large radius to the leading edge. This chain is very durable but requires a lot of power.

Semi-Chisel chain is essentially a streamlined chipper design. It features a tapered top plate, a relieved side plate and a smaller radius to the leading edge. This great-

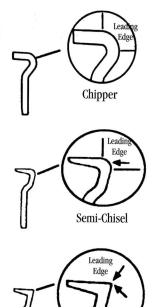

Saw Chain Cutter Designs

TechTip

It's best to match the chain to the cutting conditions. Chipper chain is the most durable but obsolete for saws under 100CC. Chisel chain is popular, but the leading edge "point" on chisel chain allows it to cut faster while sacrificing durability. Once the point becomes damaged, the chain will not cut well. This makes chisel chain a poor choice for abrasive conditions. For most applications semi-chisel chain is the best compromise of speed and durability. The leading edge is larger, rounded and, as a result, more durable.

ly increases cutting efficiency without sacrificing much durability.

Chisel chain is designed for all-out performance by making the leading edge a pointed square corner. The bottom graphic shows that the chisel chain's squared cutter also cuts faster by severing all of the wood fibers in the kerf in one pass. The actual leading edge "point" does most of the cutting and is easily damaged in abrasive conditions. As a result, chisel chain is best suited for clean, standing timber.

Saw Chain Maintenance

Products requiring routine maintenance—and saw chain falls into this category—should always be serviced according to the manufacturers recommendations. The cutting angles and depth gauge settings of saw chain installed at the factory have proven the best for a wide range of cutting conditions. Maintaining your saw chain to factory specifications will ensure chain life and cutting efficiency.

Two things must be done to properly maintain a saw chain: sharpen the cutters and lower the depth gauges. One without the other is less than effective.

As you will learn, there's a big difference between filing a chain and sharpening a chain. It's a fact that in most cases less than half of the life and cutting efficiency built into saw chain is ever realized. This is primarily due to poor and improper maintenance. To be more specific, 90 percent of all saw chain failures are directly related to improperly maintained depth gauges.

Some operators believe that they get full life from a saw chain when it's been used long enough to have the cutter teeth filed very short. Rather than using tooth length as a yard stick for chain life, a different and more practical approach is to judge chain life in terms of production, performance, self-feeding and sharpness. Understanding backslope, hook, high depth gauges and low depth gauges is an important step to correcting any maintenance-related problem.

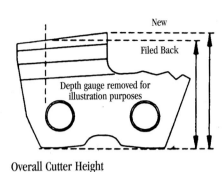

New

Filed Back

Depth gauge removed for illustration purposes

Overall Cutter Height

Sharpening Cutters

Cutters lose their sharp edge and become dull from extended cutting, abrasives in the wood (sand, ashes, etc.) or from hitting foreign objects such as dirt, nails, rocks and pavement. A good sharpening job restores each cutter's leading edge with specific filing angles recommended by the factory. The leading edge is the most important part of the cutter because it does most of the work. But this is only part of the job.

As a cutter is repeatedly sharpened, the tooth gets shorter simply because it is being filed away. Due to the "clearance angle" designed into the top plate of the cutter, the overall cutter height of the leading edge determines the size of the bite that the tooth can take. Consequently, the depth gauge must be lowered in proportion to the decreased cutter height to keep the saw chain self-feeding into the wood.

The purpose of sharpening cutters is to remove any damaged area and to restore the leading edge of the cutter. A good sharpening job leaves 1) a clean line of chrome plate on the leading edge to maintain sharpness, 2) a leading edge that is thin enough to cut efficiently, but well-supported to give it durability, 3) consistently accurate top plate angles, and 4) a clear gullet for chip clearance. It is important to avoid backslope and hook, the two most common sharpening errors.

Backslope

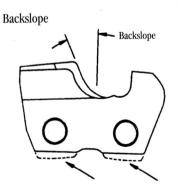

Backslope

A backsloped cutter is filed so that there is no leading edge. Backslope is caused by using a file that is too large for the chain or by holding the file up too high into the tooth when filing.

As a backsloped cutter tries to enter the wood, the blunt edge will not bite, even with the proper depth gauge setting. There is no rocking motion because the cutter only skids along the bar on its heel. The operator applies more feed pressure causing increased wear on the bottoms of the cutters and tie straps, which can lead to eventual chain breakage. He resharpens using the same technique, achieves

the same results and, over time, may come to the wrong conclusion that the chain must be "soft" because the cutters have worn heels and will not stay sharp.

A cutter with hook can be compared to a razor blade. They both cut aggressively but will get dull very quickly because the actual cutting edge has very little metal underneath to support it. Hooked cutters are caused by using a file that is too small for the chain or by holding the file too low.

A chain with hooked cutters will cut more aggressively for a while but will not stay sharp for very long. After the cutter becomes dull, the chain stops cutting. The operator applies more feed pressure causing the bottoms of the chain to wear

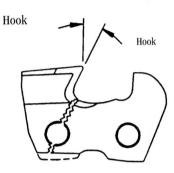

Hook

Hook

against the bar rails. In addition, hooked cutters on a partially worn chain can weaken the cutter in the gullet area, causing possible breakage. If the operator continues to refile, and not resharpen, it will compound the problem and result in poor stay-sharp, rough cutting breakage, stretch and complaints that the chain is soft.

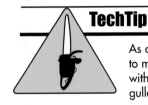

TechTip

As a cutter is filed down, it's important to make an occasional freehand stroke with the file to clear material out of the gullet that could get in the way of a good sharpening job.

Maintaining Depth Gauges

The most misunderstood part of saw chain maintenance is how far to file the depth gauges down each time the cutter is sharpened. If the depth gauges are not lowered enough, the chain will not cut efficiently. If the depth gauges are lowered too far, the chain will cut very rough. As mentioned before, depth gauges determine the size of the bite that the cutter can take.

Because of the "clearance angle" built into the top plate of the cutter, the overall height of the tooth becomes lower as it is filed back and becomes shorter in length. Therefore the depth gauge must be constantly lowered in the same proportion, gradually lowering the height of the cutter as it is filed back.

As the illustrations to the right demonstrate, a new cutter (#1) has a perfect depth gauge setting and will feed efficiently into the wood. Cutter #2 has been partially filed back without lowering the depth gauge. This cutter cannot feed into the wood because it has no depth gauge setting. In fact, the depth gauge in cutter #2 will actually hold the cutter tooth away from the wood. Cutter #3 has the same cutter length and height as cutter #2, but the depth gauge has been lowered to compensate for the shorter cutter height. As a result, cutter #3 will cut as efficiently as cutter #1.

The most common problems with depth gauges are either high depth gauges or low depth gauges. Both will be addressed here.

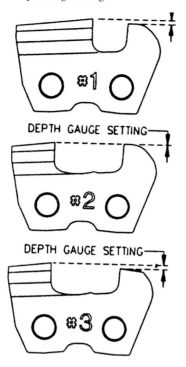

Depth Gauge Settings

DEPTH GAUGE SETTING

DEPTH GAUGE SETTING

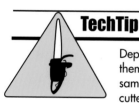

TechTip

Depth gauges do not wear down by themselves. They are made from the same hardened steel as the rest of the cutter. Depth gauges must be filed down as the cutter is filed and be shorter in length and lower in height to keep the chain self-feeding into the wood.

High depth gauges exist when the overall height of the depth gauge is nearly equal to or higher than the overall height of the cutter's leading edge. High depth gauges are caused by not filing depth gauges down enough or by not filing them down at all. This is a common problem because many operators do not know that depth gauges need to be lowered.

A unique thing happens when a sharpened cutter tries to cut with a high depth gauge. Rather than entering the wood straight on, the high depth gauge forces the wood to scrape at the leading edge of the cutter. Imagine scraping at wood with a pocket knife instead of whittling it. The blade dulls quickly. The same effect is found on saw chain with depth gauges that are too high.

The illustration at the right shows what actually happens when a cutter has a high depth gauge. The high depth gauge

directs the cutter away from the wood as shown by the top row of arrows. When the chain stops cutting, the operator pushes down, adding more feed pressure, represented by the bottom row of arrows. The chain is forced into the wood in an attempt to make it cut, as represented by the middle row of arrows into the gullet area. This operator-induced feed pressure causes the cutter bottoms to wear quickly and shows why it takes so much effort to make a chain with high depth gauges cut wood.

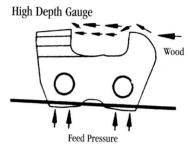

High Depth Gauge

Wood

Feed Pressure

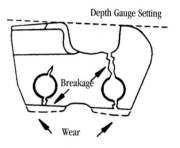

Depth Gauge Setting

Breakage

Wear

The wear pattern on saw chain with high depth gauges is similar to that of backsloped cutters because of the excessive feed pressure necessary to force the chain into the wood. The dotted area in the illustration shows this wear on the bottoms of the cutters and tie straps. This operator-induced feed pressure from high depth gauges breaks down the protective film of the bar and chain oil. The friction created also causes the bar to wear and, if left uncorrected, will lead to chain and bar failure.

Low depth gauges exist when the gauges are filed down too far below the height of the leading edge of the cutter. This causes the rocking motion to become very rough and forces the cutter to take an over-sized bite. This oversized bite causes the cutter heel to crash on to the guide bar rails. Instead of a smooth transition into the wood, the cutter grabs the wood and can literally stall in the cut. This happens because the saw motor often lacks the power to pull the cutter through the oversized bite it has taken. The cutter eventually breaks out of the wood and crashes back onto the bar. This roughness in the rocking motion can be felt as a vibration in the saw han-

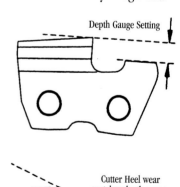

Depth Gauge Setting

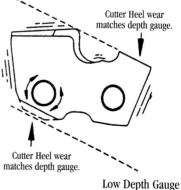

Cutter Heel wear matches depth gauge.

Cutter Heel wear matches depth gauge.

Low Depth Gauge

dles while cutting, and the saw is almost pulled from the operator's hands. An extreme low depth gauge situation can actually stall the engine.

Low depth gauges decrease the life of a saw chain significantly. The crashing motion leads to chipped cutter bottoms, tight joints where the chain is riveted together and eventual breakage. The guide bar rails bear the brunt of the pounding, which results in chipped and cracked bar rails. These failures can lead to the mistaken conclusion that the chain and/or bar are made from bad steel. A more costly by-product of uncorrected low depth gauges are chain saw engine problems including broken crankshafts, clutches and main bearings.

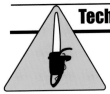

TechTip

A saw should cut without having to push down. If you have to apply force to make it cut, check the depth gauges on the saw chain. Saw chains with high depth gauges will not cut well, will not stay sharp and, if uncorrected, will ultimately lead to saw chain and guide bar failure.

Chain Cuts Crooked

Saw chain will cut crooked for several reasons. Obviously, the chain gauge must match the bar groove. When guide bar rails wear uneven or the groove becomes worn, the saw chain will ride crooked in the guide bar or sit in the bar crooked, hence the crooked cut. If the bar looks like the illustrations to the right, your dealer might be able to recondition it. If not, the bar will need to be replaced. However, if the saw chain caused the bar to wear in that fashion a new bar will eventually wear the same way. Correct the problem by filing the chain properly.

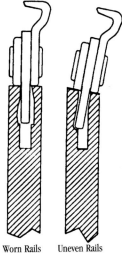

Worn Rails   Uneven Rails
Worn and Uneven Rails

Another reason for chains to cut crooked has to do with left-hand and right-hand cutters. A saw chain cutting wood is like a pick-up truck with a power-angle snowplow. Angling the plow to the left pulls the truck to the left in a snowbank, and angling the plow to the right pulls the truck to the right. When cutting wood, the left-hand cutters pull the saw chain

to the left and the right-hand cutters pull to the right. The chains cut straight because the left and right forces balance each other. Whenever one side of the chain cuts more efficiently than the other, the chain will pull in that direction. Re-sharpening the cutters and depth gauges will usually correct the problem.

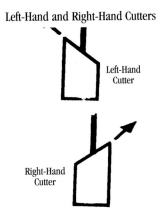

Left-Hand and Right-Hand Cutters

Left-Hand Cutter

Right-Hand Cutter

Damaged or Broken Cutters

Most quality brands of saw chain have chrome plating on the top and side plates of the cutters. This hardened industrial chrome is not shiny like a car bumper but is there to hold the sharpness of the cutter's leading edge.

Cutters that hit foreign objects become damaged and must be filed back to restore a clean line of chrome to the leading edge of the cutter. Cutters can also break from too much hook or from hitting foreign objects such as nails, spikes and barbed wire. It's important not to make the same cut once the chain has been repaired. Extreme hook and cutting frozen wood can also increase the potential for top plate breakage.

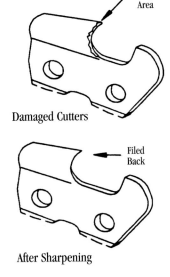

Damaged Area

Damaged Cutters

Filed Back

After Sharpening

TechTip

Manufacturers grind a top plate angle, generally 30-35 degrees, to allow for the widest range of cutting conditions. For best results, always follow the manufacturers recommendations for top plate angles.

30-35°

GUIDE BARS

This section was compiled with the cooperation of the Carlton Saw Chain Company. The technical data was supplied by Carlton in hopes that all operators of chain saws may achieve safer, more productive and better economical use of their saw chain, bars and sprockets.

Please keep in mind that each manufacturer has its own maintenance theories on its products. Check with your local Authorized Service Dealer selling the brand of product you are using. This article contains some information that pertains solely to Carlton Saw Chain.

Guide Bar Types

Guide bars are intended to serve as their name implies: to guide the saw chain. They are made of specially tempered steel. The rails of the guide bar, on which the saw chain runs, are hardened to specifications that have proven to offer the best durability in a variety of cutting conditions.

There are three types of guide bars available: solid nose, replaceable sprocket nose and laminated sprocket nose. All three can be used successfully by a chain saw carvers.

Solid-nose bars are made from a single piece of steel with a hardened surface (usually a form of Stellite®) welded to the nose area. Solid-nose bars are not intended to be used in an application that requires a lot of bore-cutting or extensive cutting with the nose portion of the bar.

Solid-Nose Guide Bar

Sprocket-nose bars have a series of needle bearings inside a sprocket wheel at the tip. A sprocket-nose is inserted into the main body of the bar and is encased in a replaceable tip that can be changed as necessary. Sprocket nose bars are designed for bore-cutting and extensive cutting. In bore-cutting, this bearing assembly takes the friction from the chain away from the body of the bar.

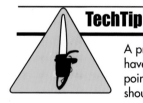

Replaceable Sprocket-Nose Guide Bar

Some sprocket-nose bars are made from a single piece of steel, like solid-nose bars. Others are "laminated bars," which means that they are made from three pieces of steel sandwiched together and spot-welded. Laminated bars are usually the most

Laminated Sprocket-Nose Guide Bar

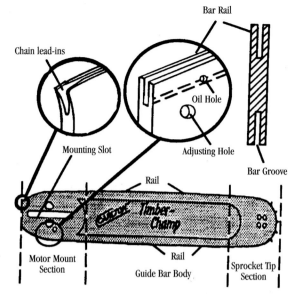

Guide Bar Components

economical to buy.

What type of bar should you use? As with any tool, it is always best to match the bar to the job. Solid-nose bars are best in gritty conditions because they have no bearings in the tip. Solid-nose bars are expensive and will wear out quickly if the nose is used extensively. Sprocket-nose bars are best for all-around cutting. For occasional to semi-professional use, laminated sprocket-nose bars are probably the best compromise for the money.

TechTip

A properly tensioned saw chain should have a small amount of sag at the midpoint of a solid nose bar. The chain should snap back tight onto the rails of a sprocket nose bar.

Guide Bar Problems

Under normal use, when saw chains are properly maintained, a guide bar should last through the life of several chains. When a guide bar does fail, it generally fails from poor saw chain maintenance, poor chain tension, lack of lubrication on the rails and/or at the tip or misuse.

Common sense dictates that guide bars should not be used as pry bars, anvils or directional felling wedges. Unfortunately, many guide bars are used for just these purposes. This misuse results in many of the most common guide bar problems.

Whenever a saw chain stops cutting (due to high depth gauges, dull cutters, etc.) the natural tendency is to push down and force the chain to cut. This turns the guide bar

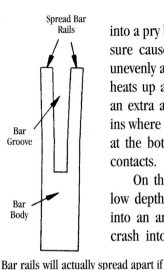

Spread Bar
Rails

Bar
Groove

Bar
Body

Bar rails will actually spread apart if run for an extended time under poor conditions. The operator may think he has a defective or soft bar, but the problem is usually in the way that the chain has been filed. If the chain problem is left uncorrected, bar failures will continue.

into a pry bar. The added friction and pressure causes the rails of the bar to wear unevenly and/or spread apart. As the chain heats up and expands (stretches) there is an extra amount of pounding at the lead-ins where the chain enters the bar rails and at the bottom of the tip where the chain contacts.

On the other hand, a saw chain with low depth gauges will turn the guide bar into an anvil. The bottoms of the cutters crash into the bar and cause chips and cracks in the bar rails as well as in the bottoms of the cutters and tie straps. This may give the operator the false impression that the bar is defective or is brittle, but the problem is in the way the chain has been filed. Once again, failure to correct the problem will ultimately lead to more chain and bar failures.

However, the number one reason by far for guide bar failure is poor maintenance.

Guide Bar Maintenance

Guide bars actually require very little maintenance. Oiling the bar and chain and conducting an inspection of the bar on a regular basis and correcting any problems will keep your guide bar in good running order.

Always use good quality bar and chain oil. This oil is blended from clean, fresh extreme-pressure-based oil with a "stay-on" additive often called PARATAC. Waste engine oil should not be used to lubricate saw chain. It contains grit and acids that can harm the saw oiler and increase bar and chain wear.

When operating properly, the saw oiler should pump enough oil so that a small amount "slings" off the end of the bar. This does not mean there is too much oil on the saw. The excess flushes away grit that could ruin the bearings of

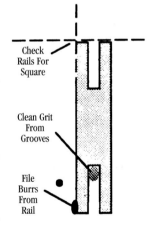

Check Rails For Square

Clean Grit From Grooves

File Burrs From Rail

the chain and accelerate bar rail wear. The oil that remains lubricates the bar and chain.

Conduct a routine inspection of the condition of your guide bar on a regular basis; every month if you do a lot of chain saw carving, less if you carve infrequently.

First, look for burrs on the rails. File them down using a flat file and light strokes. Check for cracks and twists.

Make sure the oil holes and grooves are free of sawdust and grit that can restrict lubrication.

Next, the bar rails must be even. This can be checked on a flat surface. If the bar won't stand on its rails, it needs to be "trued up." Any authorized chain saw dealer can do this for you. Lastly, the groove must be straight and deep enough for the drive links. As the rails wear, the depth of the groove becomes shallow. Insert the chain into the bar and check that the depth is sufficient. If you have any questions about the condition of the guide bar you are using, ask a dealer. Using a guide bar that has been compromised in any way could pose serious safety hazards.

DRIVE SPROCKETS

The power from the chain saw's engine is transferred to the saw chain through a centrifugal clutch and drive sprocket. There are two types of drive sprockets used on chain saws: spur sprockets and rim sprockets. Spur sprockets incorporate the centrifugal clutch drum and drive sprocket into a single piece and must be changed as a complete unit. Rim sprockets are a two-piece unit that allows you to change just the rim as it wears out. Originally, all saws used spur sprockets. The rim sprocket design came along in recent years. Both work well, although some chain saw carvers prefer one over the other.

Regardless of the

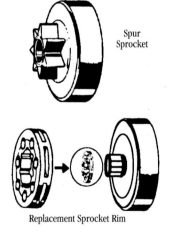

Spur Sprocket

Replacement Sprocket Rim

design, there are two things that you need to know about drive sprockets. 1.) The drive sprocket pitch must match the pitch of the saw chain and guide bar (sprocket nose bar). 2.) The drive sprocket must be replaced when worn out.

Drive Sprocket Wear

The saw chain and drive sprocket are a matched set—just like two gears working together. As the chain wears out, the drive sprocket wears out too. If the drive sprocket is not replaced on a regular basis (preferably with every new chain), the new chain will wear to match the amount of wear that is in the sprocket. The result is called "stretch."

For example, a common .325 pitch sprocket has seven teeth. The .325 pitch sprocket matches a .325 pitch saw chain. If the sprocket has only .010" of wear (about the thickness of a match), the effective wear on the sprocket is actually .070" when the sprocket is turning at 12,000 rpm engine speed. That makes the .325 sprocket with .070" wear a .395 sprocket! A new .325 pitch chain on this sprocket will try to "stretch" match the wear in the sprocket drive teeth.

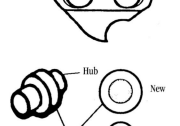

Drive Link and Rivet Flange Wear
What usually appears to be chain "stretch" is actually wear. The diagrams show this wear in the drive links and rivet flanges. The new chain tries to mesh into the worn or improper pitch sprocket.

The flanges of the rivets are specially heat-treated to be a bearing surface against the insides of the drive link holes. When the chain tries to mesh into a worn or improper pitch drive sprocket, tremendous stresses occur in this area of the chain. This mismatch causes the chain to wear in an attempt to match the pitch of the sprocket.

Worn or improper pitch sprockets also show wear patterns on other parts of the chain. Each type of sprocket leaves different marks because of the way the chain is driven. Spurs contact the chain in the notches below the cutters and tie straps. The wear from drive sprocket problems shows up in that area. Rims actually push the chain along

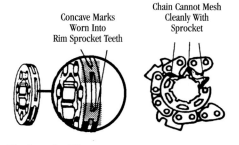

Rim Sprocket Wear

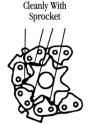
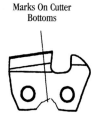

Spur Sprocket Wear

from behind the drive links. This leaves less obvious marks but the same outcome—stretch and breakage.

Sometimes the rivet bearings and drive link holes can wear to the point of the operator having to shorten the chain by removing drive links in order to maintain chain tension. Worn sprockets cause the joints of the chain to tighten up and, in extreme cases, will literally tear the chain into pieces.

Installing a new drive sprocket is the best way to avoid the rivet bearing and drive link wear that appears as chain stretch.

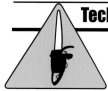

TechTip

Extreme cold weather can accelerate all forms of chain and bar failures, but particularly those from sprocket-related problems. All steel parts become more brittle and less tolerant of shock loads and stress as the temperature drops below freezing.

Drive Sprocket Maintenance

It's a fact that at least five out of ten saws in use today probably need new sprockets. It's a part of the chain saw that's out of sight and not given a lot of attention. However, the kinds of problems that worn sprockets or sprockets with improper pitch create make it worth checking every time the chain is replaced.

A quick and easy way to test for a worn sprocket is to shut the saw off and pull the chain around the bar under proper tension. If it pulls roughly or feels "ratchety" the sprocket is probably worn. Sometimes a worn sprocket makes it impossible to tension the chain without it binding up!

Another thing to remember is that when it comes to sprockets, what matters most is not how old it is, but how worn it is. For example, a new sprocket can become worn very quickly if the chain falls off and damages the sprocket due to improper installation. The sprocket would need to be changed even though it's still almost new.

Remember, the sprocket must match the pitch of the

chain and guide bar tip. As with saw chain and guide bar complaints, "stretch" and the problems associated with it can be avoided. Here are a few tips to remember.

- Always install a new chain on a new sprocket of proper pitch.
- Periodically check drive sprockets for wear.
- Replace drive sprockets at the first visible sign of wear.

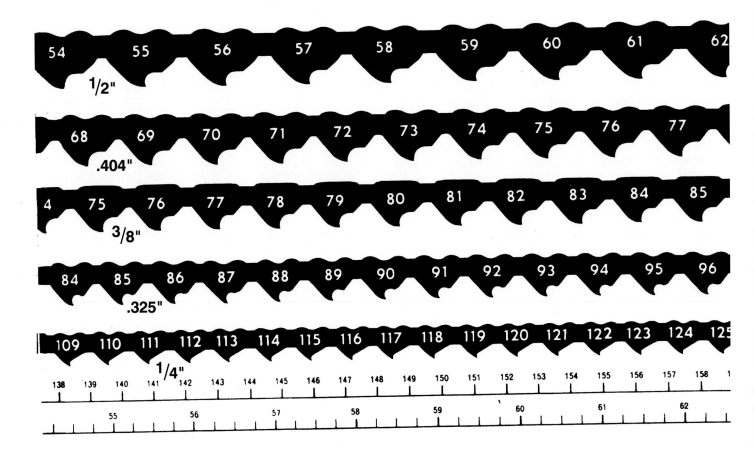

A bench chart, such as this one by Carlton, will help you identify the pitch of your saw chain. Simply lay your saw chain on the chart and match up the tips of the drive links to the compatible, corresponding illustration on the chart. Low profile $3/8$ in. pitch and standard $3/8$ in. are the same spread. The measurements below each chain indicate pitch. The white numbers over the chain indicate the number of drive links at a given measurement on the bench chart.

1999–2000 Chain Saw Specifications Chart

The following Chain Saw Specifications Chart was reprinted with the express permission of *Power Equipment Trade Magazine,* a Hatton-Brown Publication, Montgomery, Alabama *Power Equipment Trade Magazine* updates these figures yearly. The chart can be used to compare information for a number of chain saws available on today's market.

Model	Engine CC	HP/kW	Powerhead	Fuel capacity	Oil capacity	Anti-vibe	Oil system	Carb type (mfg./model no.)	Safety Features	Fuel mix	Bar length	Sugg. Retail
DESA International, Box 90004, Bowling Green, KY 42102-9004 (502-781-9600)												
076728K	—	1.25	3.4	—	1.25	N	M	—	A,B	—	12	$49.99
075762J	—	2.5	5.4	—	1.25	N	M	—	A,B	—	14	$59.99
099178H	—	1.5	3.8	—	1.25	N	M	—	A,B	—	14	$54.99
098031J	—	3.25	5.4	—	1.25	N	M	—	A,B	—	16	$69.99
100089-05	—	3.25	5.4	—	1.25	N	M	—	A,B	—	16	$69.99
100089-06	—	1.5	4.4	—	1.25	N	M	—	A,B	—	14	$59.99
104317*	—	1.25	10	—	1.25	N	M	—	A,B	—	8	$99.99
*Electric pole saw												
Dolmar USA, 14930 Northam St., LaMirada, CA 90638 (888-673-7278)												
PS 3300-TH	32	1.6/1.2	7.3	7.8	5.0	Y	A	W/WT-407	A,B,C	50:1	12-16	—
PS 34	33	1.8/1.3	8.8	12.5	8.5	Y	A	Zama	A,B,C	50:1	14-16	—
PS 341	33	1.9/1.4	8.6	13.3	8.5	Y	A	W/WT-174	A,B,C	50:1	14-16	—
PS 401	39	2.3/1.7	8.8	13.3	8.5	Y	A	W/WT-174	A,B,C	50:1	14-16	—
109	43	2.8/2.0	10.2	18.6	9.3	Y	A	W/WT-76	A,B,C	50:1	15-18	—
111	52	3.3/2.4	10.4	18.6	9.0	Y	A	T/HU-83	A,B,C	50:1	18-20	—
PS 540	54	3.4/2.5	10.4	18.6	9.0	Y	A	W/WT 374	A,B,C	50:1	18-21	—
PS 6000i	60	4.6/3.1	13.2	30.0	13.5	Y	A	T/HS-236	A,B,C	50:1	18-24	—
PS 6800i	68	5.1/3.7	13.8	30.0	13.5	Y	A	T/HS-236	C	50:1	18-28	—
PS 9010	90	6.7/4.9	17.4	33.7	12.5	Y	A	T/HS-294A	C	50:1	18-32	—
Echo Inc., 400 Oakwood Rd., Lake Zurich, IL 60047 (847-540-8400)												
CS-3000	30.1	—	7.5	8.5	5.0	Y	A	W/WT Series	A,B,C,D	50:1	12-16	$229.99
CS-3450	33.4	—	8	8.5	5.0	Y	A	W/WT Series	A,B,C,D	50:1	12-16	$279.99
CS-5000	49.3	—	11.3	15.9	9.8	Y	A	W/HDA Series	A,B,C,D	50:1	16-20	$399.99
CS-6700	66.7	—	13.2	21.0	10.5	Y	A/M	W/HDA Series	A,C,D	50:1	16-27	$699.99
CS-8000	80.7	—	16.3	27.7	13.5	Y	A/M	W/HDA Series	A,C,D	50:1	20-36	$899.99
CS-3400	33.4	—	7.6	8.5	5.0	Y	A	W/WT Series	A,B,C,D	50:1	12-16	$249.99
CS-4400	43.6	—	10.5	20.3	9.5	Y	A	W/WT Series	A,B,C,D	50:1	16-20	$379.99
ECS-2000	—	2.0	6.0	—	1.25	—	M	—	A,B,C,D	—	12	$99.99
ECS-3000	—	3.25	7.5	—	1.25	—	M	—	A,B,C,D	—	16	$119.99
Frigidaire Home Products (Poulan), 250 Bobby Jones Expressway, Augusta, GA 30907 (706-651-1751)												
2050	33	—	10.4	12.8	6.8	N	A	W	A,B	40:1	14	$129.99
2150	34	—	10.4	12.8	6.8	N	A	W	A,B	40:1	16	$149.99
2175	35	—	10.4	12.8	6.8	N	A	W	A,B	40:1	18	$159.99
2250	36	—	10.8	12.8	7.4	Y	A	W	A,B	40:1	16	$169.99
2450	38	—	10.8	12.8	7.4	Y	A	W	A,B	40:1	16-18	$179.99

Model	Engine CC	HP/KW	Powerhead	Fuel capacity	Oil capacity	Anti-vibe	Oil system	Carb type (mfg./model no.)	Safety Features	Fuel mix	Bar length	Sugg. Retail
757	73.5	5.6	14.9	25.7	11.1	Y	A	W/HDA-123	Y	40:1	18-32	$712.95
577	57.3	4.0	13.0	23.7	11.2	Y	A	W/HDA-132	Y	40:1	18-24	$540.17
357*	35.5	1.8	9.1	9.3	7.6	Y	A	W/WT-301B	Y	40:1	12-16	$327.98
757C	73.5	5.6	14.9	25.7	11.1	Y	A	W/HDA	Y	40:1	18-32	$692.95

*High torque model

Solo Inc., Box 5030, Newport News, VA 23605 (757-245-4228)

Model	Engine CC	HP/KW	Powerhead	Fuel capacity	Oil capacity	Anti-vibe	Oil system	Carb type (mfg./model no.)	Safety Features	Fuel mix	Bar length	Sugg. Retail
636	36	2.0/1.5	8.4	13.8	7.1	Y	A	W	A,B,C	50:1	14-16	$269.95
639	38	2.6/1.9	9.9	17	9.1	Y	A	W	A,B,C	50:1	16-18	$329.95
645	44	3.0/2.2	9.9	17	9.1	Y	A	W	A,B,C	50:1	16-20	$379.95
651	51	4.0/2.9	10.7	22.4	12.8	Y	A	W	A,B,C	50:1	16-20	$599.95
651-SP	51	3.6/2.65	10.7	22.4	12.8	Y	A	W	A,B,C	50:1	16-20	$425.95
662	62	4.3/3.2	13.8	28.0	13.2	Y	A	W/HDA	A,B,C	50:1	16-28	$689.95
690D/690WD	80	7.3/5.4	16.7	29.3	15.3	Y	A	W/WJ	A,B,C	50:1	16-42	$819.95

Stihl Inc., 536 Viking Dr., Virginia Beach, VA 23452 (757-486-9100)

Model	Engine CC	HP/KW	Powerhead	Fuel capacity	Oil capacity	Anti-vibe	Oil system	Carb type (mfg./model no.)	Safety Features	Fuel mix	Bar length	Sugg. Retail
009 Mini Boss	36.6	1.61	9.0	9.8	7.8	Y	A	—	A,B,C	50:1	12-16	$229.95
017	30.1	1.6	8.6	8.5	5.1	Y	A	—	A,B,C	50:1	12-14	$199.95
018C	31.8	1.8	8.6	8.5	5.1	Y	A	---	A,B,C	50:1	12-16	$199.95
019T	35.2	1.7	8.8	9.8	5.4	Y	A	—	A,B,C	50:1	12-16	$259.95
020 T	35.2	2.2	7.9	8.2	8.2	Y	A	—	A,B,C	50:1	12-16	$499.95
021 Wood Boss	35.2	1.8	9.9	16.0	6.4	Y	A	—	A,B,C	50:1	12-16	$249.95
023L	40.2	1.5	10.3	16.0	6.4	Y	A	—	A,B,C	50:1	12-14	$299.95
023C	40.2	2.6	10.3	16.0	6.4	Y	A	—	A,B,C	50:1	12-16	$299.95
025 Wood Boss	44.3	3.0	10.3	16.0	6.4	Y	A	—	A,B,C	50:1	12-18	$299.95
026 Pro	48.7	3.5	10.6	16.0	10.9	Y	A	—	A,B,C	50:1	16-24	$429.95
029 Super Farm Boss	57.0	3.75	13.2	18.9	11.2	Y	A	—	A,B,C	50:1	16-24	$299.95
036 Pro	61.5	4.4	12.5	21.1	10.9	Y	A	—	A,B,C	50:1	16-28	$549.95
036 QS	61.5	4.6	13.3	21.1	10.9	Y	A	—	A,B,C,D	50:1	16-28	$699.95
039	64.1	4.3	13.2	18.9	11.2	Y	A	—	A,B,C	50:1	16-28	$449.95
044	70.7	5.1	13.5	27.2	11.2	Y	A	—	A,B,C	50:1	16-32	$674.95
044 Arctic	70.7	5.1	13.5	27.2	11.2	Y	A	—	A,B,C	50:1	16-32	$744.95
046 Magnum	76.5	5.9	14.4	32.0	12.8	Y	A	—	A,B,C	50:1	16-32	$724.95
046 M Arctic	76.5	5.9	14.4	32.0	12.8	Y	A	—	A,B,C	50:1	16-32	$794.95
066 Magnum	91.6	7.0	16.3	28.3	11.8	Y	A	—	A,B,C	50:1	16-36	$884.95
088 Magnum	121.6	8.5	22.2	41.6	21.3	Y	A	—	A,B,C	50:1	21-47	$1,494.95
E140	—	1.9	7.0	—	—	Y	A	—	A,B,C	50:1	12-14	$294.95
E180 C	—	2.3	7.7	—	—	Y	A	—	A,B,C	50:1	14-18	$344.95
E220	—	2.3	10.8	---	—	---	—	---	A,B,C	---	16-20	$499.95
HT70	25.4	1.2	11.8	15.4	8.2	Y	A	—	A,B	50:1	12-14	$449.95
HT75 Pruner	25.4	1.2	15.8	—	—	Y	A	—	A,B	50:1	12-14	$599.95

Tanaka, 22461 72nd Ave. S., Kent, WA 98032 (253-395-3900)

Model	Engine CC	HP/KW	Powerhead	Fuel capacity	Oil capacity	Anti-vibe	Oil system	Carb type (mfg./model no.)	Safety Features	Fuel mix	Bar length	Sugg. Retail
ECS-3301	32.3	1.6	7.3	7.8	5.0	Y	A	W	A,B,C	50:1	12-14	$299.99
ECS-3351	32.3	1.6	7.7	7.8	5.0	Y	A	W	A,B,C	50:1	12-14	$309.99
ECV-4501	43	2.6	9.0	13.5	8.3	Y	A	W	A,B,C	50:1	16-20	$389.99
TCS-3401	34	1.8	7.9	10.1	6.4	Y	A	W	A,B,C	50:1	12-16	$339.99
TPS-2510*	24	1.3	11.4	19.3	5.4	Y	A	W	A,B,C	50:1	10	$399.99

*Pole chain saw

Model	Engine CC	HP/AW	Powerhead	Fuel capacity	Oil capacity	Anti-vibe	Oil system	Carb type (mfg./model no.)	Safety Features	Fuel mix	Bar length	Sugg. Retail
2550	40	—	10.8	12.8	7.4	Y	A	W	A,B	40:1	18	$189.99
2750/2900	46	—	10	13.9	9.8	Y	A	W	A,B	40:1	18-20	$209.99
3300	54	—	11.6	20	10	Y	A	W	A,B	40:1	20	$259.99
3450	54	—	12.6	20	10	Y	A	W	A,B	40:1	20	$269.99
3500	60	—	12	20	10	Y	A	W	A,B	40:1	20	$289.99
3750	60	—	13	20	10	Y	A	W	A,B	40:1	22	$309.99
Poulan Pro												
PP S-23 Arbor Pro	38	—	9	11.5	6.5	N	A	W	A,B,C	40:1	14	$229.99
PP210	36	—	11.1	12.8	6.8	N	A	W	A,B,C	40:1	16	$169.99
PP260	42	—	11.2	12.8	7.4	Y	A	W	A,B,C	40:1	18	$189.99
PP 295	45	—	10.8	13.9	9.8	Y	A	W	A,B,C	40:1	18	$259.99
PP 380	60	—	13	20.3	10.4	Y	A	W	B,C	40:1	20	$399.99
PP335	54	—	12.0	20.3	10.4	Y	A	W	A,B,C	40:1	20	$349.99
PP 445	71	—	14.9	28.6	13.6	Y	A	W	C	40:1	16-36	$699.99
PP 505	83	—	14.9	28.8	13.6	Y	A	W	C	40:1	20-36	$799.99

Greenlee Textron*, 4455 Boeing Dr., Rockford, IL 61109-2988 (815-397-7070)

Model	Engine CC	HP/AW	Powerhead	Fuel capacity	Oil capacity	Anti-vibe	Oil system	Carb type (mfg./model no.)	Safety Features	Fuel mix	Bar length	Sugg. Retail
H6200B	—	—	10	—	—	N	A	—	A	—	18	$1,150.00
43179	—	—	7	—	—	N	A	—	A	—	16	$1,115.00
43178	—	—	8	—	—	N	A	—	A	—	16	$1,345.00
38568	—	—	9	—	—	N	A	—	A	—	16	$1,370.00
43177	—	—	9	—	—	N	A	—	A	—	16	$1,395.00

*All models are hydraulic.

Homelite Inc., 14401 Carowinds Blvd., Charlotte, NC 28273 (704-588-3200)

Model	Engine CC	HP/AW	Powerhead	Fuel capacity	Oil capacity	Anti-vibe	Oil system	Carb type (mfg./model no.)	Safety Features	Fuel mix	Bar length	Sugg. Retail
20	33	—	10	18.6	11.8	N	A	Z	A,B,D	50:1	14-16	$159.99
d3300	33	—	10	18.6	11.8	N	A	Z	A,B,D	50:1	14-16	$159.99
23AV	38	—	11	18.6	11.8	Y	A	Z	A,B,C,D	50:1	16-18	$179.99
d3850b	38	—	11	18.6	11.8	Y	A	Z	A,B,C,D	50:1	16-18	$179.99
27AV	45	—	11	18.6	11.8	Y	A	Z	A,B,C,D	50:1	18-20	$219.99
d4550b	45	—	11	18.6	11.8	Y	A	Z	A,B,C,D	50:1	18-20	$219.99

*Note: All units can be purchased with or without a carry case.

Husqvarna, 9006-J Perimeter Woods Dr., Charlotte, NC 28216 (704-597-5000)

Model	Engine CC	HP/AW	Powerhead	Fuel capacity	Oil capacity	Anti-vibe	Oil system	Carb type (mfg./model no.)	Safety Features	Fuel mix	Bar length	Sugg. Retail
Electric 16	—	2.2/1.6	8.2	—	2.9	Y	A	—	A,B,C	—	12-16	$229.95
335XPT	35	2.2/1.6	7.5	13.5	8.4	Y	A	W	A,B,C	50:1	12-16	$389.95
136	36	2.2/1.6	10.1	13.5	6.8	Y	A	W	A,B,C	50:1	14-18	$199.95
141	40	2.6/1.9	10.1	13.5	6.8	Y	A	W	A,B,C	50:1	14-18	$219.95
340	41	2.7/2.0	10.4	17.0	8.3	Y	A	W	A,B,C	50:1	13-18	$269.95
345	45	3.0/2.2	10.4	17.0	8.3	Y	A	W	A,B,C	50:1	13-18	$289.95
350	50	3.1/2.3	10.6	17.0	8.3	Y	A	W	A,B,C	50:1	15-20	$329.95
351	50	3.1/2.3	10.6	17.0	8.3	Y	A	W	A,B,C	50:1	15-20	$379.95
346XP	45	3.4/2.5	10.6	17.0	8.3	Y	A	W	A,B,C	50:1	13-18	$399.95
51	51	3.1/2.3	11.6	20.3	10.1	Y	A	Z	A,B,C	50:1	15-20	$299.95
55 Rancher	53	3.3/2.4	11.4	20.3	10.1	Y	A	Z	A,B,C	50:1	18-20	$299.95
55	53	3.4/2.5	11.4	20.3	10.1	Y	A	Z	A,B,C	50:1	15-20	$339.95
261	62	4.2/3.0	12.8	20.3	10.4	Y	A	W	A,B,C	50:1	16-24	$449.95
362XP	62	4.6/3.4	13.0	25.6	15.2	Y	A	W	A,B,C	50:1	16-24	$579.95
365	65	4.6/3.4	13.0	25.6	15.2	Y	A	Z	A,B,C	50:1	16-24	$539.95
371XP	71	5.4/4.0	13.0	25.6	15.2	Y	A	W	A,B,C	50:1	16-32	$629.95
288XP Lite	88	6.1/4.5	15.9	30.4	16.9	Y	A	T	A,B,C	50:1	16-36	$699.95
394XP	94	7.1/5.2	17.0	30.4	16.9	Y	A	W	A,B,C	50:1	20-48	$929.95
3120XP	119	9.2/6.8	22.9	42.4	23.0	Y	A/M	W	A,B,C	50:1	20-60	$1,199.95

Reprinted with permission of Power Equipment Trade Magazine, a Hatton-Brown Publication, Montgomery, Alabama

Model	Engine CC	HP/kW	Powerhead	Fuel capacity	Oil capacity	Anti-vibe	Oil system	Carb type (mfg./model no.)	Safety Features	Fuel mix	Bar length	Sugg. Retail

John Deere, 14401 Carowinds Blvd., Charlotte, NC 28273 (704-588-3200)

Model	Engine CC	HP/kW	Powerhead	Fuel capacity	Oil capacity	Anti-vibe	Oil system	Carb type	Safety Features	Fuel mix	Bar length	Sugg. Retail
200cs	38	—	11	18.6	11.8	Y	A	Z	A,B,C,D	50:1	14-16	$199.99
230cs	38	—	11	18.6	11.8	Y	A	Z	A,B,C,D	50:1	16-18	$239.99

Jonsered, distributed by (Eastern U.S.): Tilton Equip. Co. (800-447-1152)
(Western U.S.): Scotsco Inc., 9160 SE 74th Ave., Portland, OR 97206 (503-777-4726)

Model	Engine CC	HP/kW	Powerhead	Fuel capacity	Oil capacity	Anti-vibe	Oil system	Carb type	Safety Features	Fuel mix	Bar length	Sugg. Retail
2036 Turbo	36	2.2/1.6	9.9	13.9	7.1	Y	A	W/WT202	A,C	50:1	16	$259.95
2040 Turbo	40	2.6/1.9	9.9	13.9	7.1	Y	A	W/WT202	A,C	50:1	16	$279.95
2045 Turbo	44.3	3.0/2.2	10.6	16.9	8.4	Y	A	Z/C1Q-EL1	A,C	50:1	13-18	$349.95
2050 Turbo	48.9	3.3/2.4	10.6	16.9	8.4	Y	A	Z/C1Q-EL1	A,C	50:1	13-20	$399.95
2054 Turbo	53.2	3.5/2.5	11.2	18.9	12.8	Y	A	W/HDA68	A,C	50:1	13-18	$499.95
2063 Turbo	62.4	4.6/3.4	13.2	25.7	13.3	Y	A	W/HD12	C	50:1	16-24	$629.95
2065 Turbo	65	4.6/3.4	13.2	23.6	13.5	Y	A	W/HD12	C	50:1	16-36	$579.95
2071 Turbo	71	5.4/4.0	13.2	25.7	13.3	Y	A	W/HD12	C	50:1	16-36	$689.95
2083II Turbo	76.5	5.4/4.0	14.9	28.7	13.5	Y	A	W/WJ77	C	50:1	16-36	$799.95
2095 Turbo	98.6	7.1/5.2	17.4	30.4	23.6	Y	A	T/HS265A	C	50:1	16-60	$894.95
2016EL	—	2.1/1.6	8.1	—	4.7	N	A	—	A,C	—	13-15	$219.95

Makita USA, 14930 Northam St., LaMirada, CA 90638 (800-4-MAKITA)

Model	Engine CC	HP/kW	Powerhead	Fuel capacity	Oil capacity	Anti-vibe	Oil system	Carb type	Safety Features	Fuel mix	Bar length	Sugg. Retail
DCS 330-TH	32	1.6/1.2	7.8	7.8	5.0	Y	A	W/WT-407	A,B,C	50:1	12-16	—
DCS 34	33	1.8/1.3	8.6	12.5	8.5	Y	A	Zama	A,B,C	50:1	14-16	—
DCS341	33	1.9/1.4	8.6	13.3	8.5	Y	A	W/WT-174	A,B,C	50:1	14-16	—
DCS401	39	2.3/1.7	8.8	13.3	8.5	Y	A	W/WT-174	A,B,C	50:1	14-16	—
DCS520	52	3.3/2.4	10.4	18.6	9.0	Y	A	T/HU-83	A,B,C	50:1	18-20	—
DCS540	54	3.4/2.5	10.4	18.6	9.0	Y	A	W/WT-374	A,B,C	50:1	18-21	—
DCS6000i-21	60	4.6/3.1	13.2	30.0	13.5	Y	A	T/HS-236	A,B,C	50:1	18-24	—
DCS6800i	68	5.1/3.7	13.8	30.0	13.5	Y	A	T/HS-236	C	50:1	18-28	—
DCS9010	90	6.7/4.9	17.4	33.7	12.5	Y	A	T/HS-294A	C	50:1	20-32	—

Olympyk, Distributed by Tilton Equip. Co., St. Paul, MN; Rye, NH; Alpharetta, GA;
Little Rock, AR (800-447-1152)

Model	Engine CC	HP/kW	Powerhead	Fuel capacity	Oil capacity	Anti-vibe	Oil system	Carb type	Safety Features	Fuel mix	Bar length	Sugg. Retail
935DF	35	1.7/1.25	8.6	9.0	5.1	Y	A	W/WT-66	A,C	50:1	12-16	$259.95
941	41.5	2.3/1.68	10.6	16.9	9.8	Y	A	W-WT162	A,C	50:1	15-18	$279.95
951	50	3.4/2.5	10.7	16.9	9.8	Y	A	W/WTA6	A,C	50:1	15-18	$329.95
962	61.5	4.7/3.5	12.1	23.7	11.8	Y	A	W/HDA146	A,C	50:1	16-24	$499.95
970	70	5.2/3.8	14.8	29	14.9	Y	A	W/UJ44	C	50:1	16-36	$549.95
980	80.7	5.7/4.2	14.5	29	14.9	Y	A	—	C	50:1	16-42	$609.95
999F	101	7.2/5.3	22	34	21	Y	A/M	T/HT4	C	50:1	16-60	$799.95

Redmax, 1505 Pavillion Pl. Suite A, Norcross, GA 30093 (770-381-5147)

Model	Engine CC	HP/kW	Powerhead	Fuel capacity	Oil capacity	Anti-vibe	Oil system	Carb type	Safety Features	Fuel mix	Bar length	Sugg. Retail
G561AVS	53.2	—	14.3	22.0	11.75	Y	A	W/HDA55B	A,B,C	32:1	16-20	$599.99
G621AVS	62	—	14.9	22.0	11.75	Y	A	W/HDA56B	A,B,C	32:1	16-24	$659.99
G310TS	30.1	—	7.3	7.5	4.5	Y	A	W/WT	A,B,C	32:1	14	$299.95
G455AVS	44.8	—	10.7	18.7	8.8	Y	A	W/WT	A,B,C	32:1	16	$469.99

Shindaiwa Inc., 11975 SW Herman Rd., Tualatin, OR 97062 (800-521-7733)

Model	Engine CC	HP/kW	Powerhead	Fuel capacity	Oil capacity	Anti-vibe	Oil system	Carb type	Safety Features	Fuel mix	Bar length	Sugg. Retail
300S	28.5	1.7	8.8	11.5	8.1	Y	A	W/WYM-1A	Y	40:1	14	$259.00
360	35.2	2.5	8.8	13.5	8.1	Y	A	W/WT-89	Y	40:1	14-16	$298.65
377*	37.7	2.5	9.0	13.5	8.1	Y	A	W/WT-229	Y	40:1	16	$369.99
488	47.9	3.5	10.1	18.1	10.1	Y	A	W/WA-79A	Y	40:1	16-20	$387.40

G R E E N L E E
Product shots provided by the manufacturer.

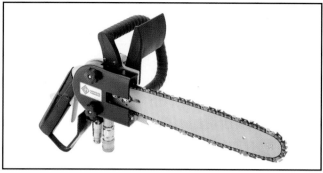

Greenlee Pistol-Grip Chain Saw

Greenlee Standard Chain Saw

H O M E L I T E
Product shots provided by the manufacturer.

Homelite 20

Homelite 23av

Homelite 27av

H U S Q V A R N A
Product shots provided by the manufacturer.

Husqvarna, model 141

Husqvarna, model 242xpg

Husqvarna, model 254xpg

Husqvarna, model 262xp

Husqvarna, model 288xplite

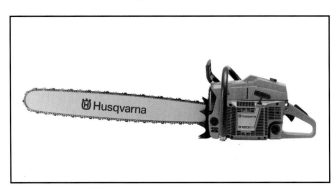

Husqvarna, model 3120xp

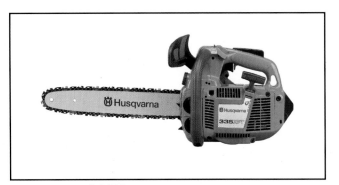

Husqvarna, model 335xpt

Husqvarna, model 340

Husqvarna, model 345

Husqvarna, model 346xp

Husqvarna, model 350

Husqvarna, model 362xp

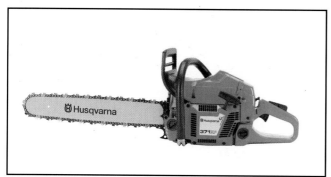

Husqvarna, model 371xp

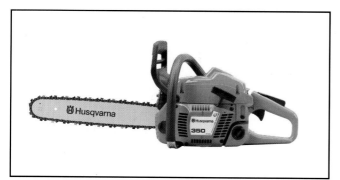

Husqvarna, model 49

Husqvarna, model 351

Husqvarna, model 365

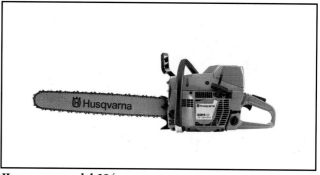

Husqvarna, model 394xp

Husqvarna, model 51

Husqvarna, model 55rancher

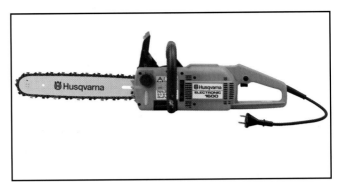

Husqvarna, model el16

Husqvarna, model 395xp

Husqvarna, model 136

JONSERED

Product shots provided by the manufacturer.

Jonsered 2149

Jonsered Pro 35

Jonsered 2016EL

Jonsered 2040

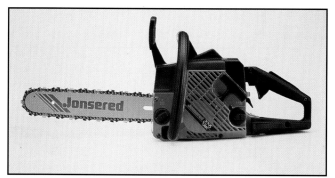

Jonsered 2045

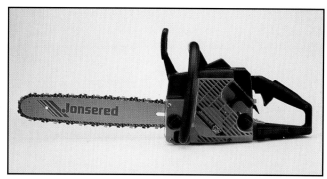

Jonsered 2050

Jonsered 2054

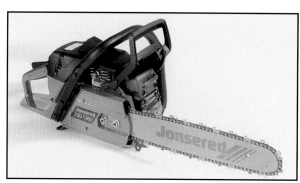

Jonsered 2063

Jonsered 2065

Jonsered 2071

Jonsered 2083

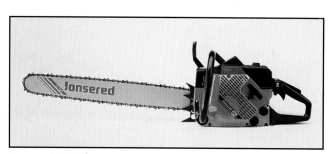

Jonsered 2095

Product shots provided by the manufacturer.

Makita DCS330TH

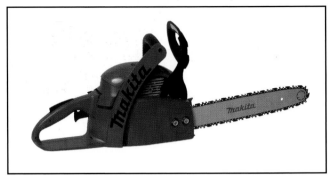

Makita DCS34

Makita DCS341

Makita DCS401

Makita DCS520

Makita DCS540

Makita DCS6000i–21

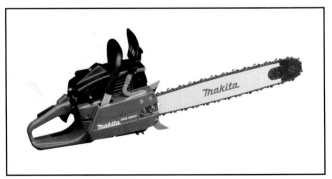

Makita DCS6800iFL

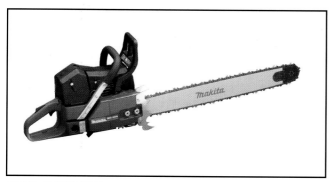

Makita DCS9010FL

O L Y M P Y K

Product shots provided by the manufacturer.

Olympyk 935DF

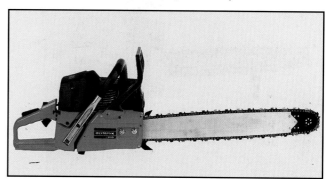

Olympyk 980

Olympyk 940

Olympyk 951

Olympyk 962

Olympyk 970

Olympyk 999

P O U L A N

Product shots provided by the manufacturer.

Poulan 2050

Poulan PP210

Poulan 2150

Poulan 2450

Poulan PP260

Poulan 2900

Poulan PP295

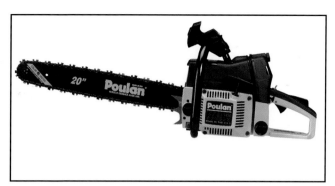

Poulan 3450

Poulan 3750

Poulan PP380

STIHL

Product shots provided by the manufacturer.

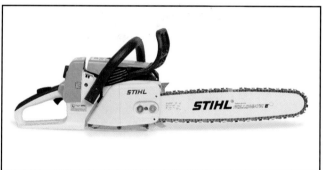

Stihl 26Pro

*kickback may result when using tip of bar

Stihl 46

*kickback may result when using tip of bar

Stihl 66

*kickback may result when using tip of bar

Product shots provided by the manufacturer.

Tanaka ECS–3301

Tanaka ECV–4501

Tanaka ECS–3351

Carver Bars

A variety of bars are available to add versatility to your chain saw. The following information was provided by GB Bars and Sprockets.

CARVER/CARPENTER BAR SPECIFICATIONS

Part No.	Nose Type	Nose Diameter	Length	Chain	# Drive Links Mount
CV12–50	Dime Tip	17 mm.	12 in.	1/4 in.	62Universal
CVY12–50	Quarter Tip	25 mm.	12 in.	3/8 in. LP	45Universal
CV18–50	Dime Tip	17 mm.	18 in.	1/4 in.	91Universal
CVY18–50	Quarter Tip	25 mm.	18 in.	3/8 in. LP	68Universal
SNCY18–50	Quarter Tip	25 mm.	18 in.	3/8 in. LP	68Stihl 024, 036, 034

CV & CVY

SNCY

CARVER/CARPENTER BAR APPLICATION CHART

Dolmar — 100, 100S, 101, 102, 103, 104, 105, 106, 108, 109, Hobby, 110, 111, 112, 113, 114, 115, 116, 117, 118, 119, 120, 219

Echo — 280, 281, 290, 291, 301, 302, 304, 315, 330, 331, 341, 351, 361, 391, 401, 3000, 3450, CS300EVL, CS302S, CS330EVL, CS400EVL, CS440, CS441, CS3900, CS4010, CS4500, CS4510

Homelite — 130, 150, 240, 245, 250, 252, 290, 300, 340, CS40, CS50, XL Mini

Husqvarna — 257, 262

John Deere — 25EV, 28, 30, 46, 450, 40V, 35EV, 45EV

Jonsered — LJ25, Pro 35, 370, 380, 410, 420, 425, 450, 451, 455, 490, 510, 520, 521, 525, 535

McCullough — all mini saws

Olympyk — 233, 234, 240, 241, 244, 335, 340, 935DF, 940, 942, 945, 946, 950, 951, OM–E200, 140EF, E300

Poulan — 255, 295, 335, 336, 1800, 2000, 2100, 2300, 2500, 2600, 2700, 2800, 3000, 25E, S25AV, S25CVA, S25DA, S25D, Micro 25

Poulan Pro — S25, 250, 225, 235, 285, 305, 325, 335

Red Max 320, 361, 375, 400, 410, 450, 455, 3400, 3700, 3800, 3900, 4000, 4200, 4900, G300TS, G300AVS, G400

Rigid 305A, 350AM, 340 Super, 380, 380AV

Shindaiwa 100, 104P, 110, 140, 150, (Electrics), 160, 180, 300, 345, 350, 360, E305AV, 415, 416, 450, 451, 485, 488, 500

Stihl 020AV, 020AVP, 09, 010, 011, 012, 015, 017, 015LE, 021, 023, 025, E10 Electric

Tanaka ECS-35, ECS-290, ECS-300, ECS-330, ECS-350, ECS-351, ECS-355, ECS-356, ECS-370, ECS-405, ECS-3500, ECS-4000B

Carver bars are also available from Bailey's Inc., a chainsaw supply company with headquarters in California and Louisiana.

A Condensed History of the Chain Saw

1600s
- Saw chain is invented for use with hand-cranked machines in Welsh coal mines.

1858-1905
- 25 patents are issued on endless or sectional cutting chains.

1858
- The first chain saw patent is issued to Harvey Brown of New York.

1878
- The first on-site, mechanized sawing device may have been a steam-driven, reciprocating saw developed by an Englishman named Ransome.

1885
- German engineer Gottlieb Daimler produces a small internal combustion engine that revolutionizes the outdoor power equipment industry.

1904
- The first saw to use a chain on a rail is developed, but no power source is lightweight enough to make it portable.

1920
- Inventor Charles Wolf designs and patents a semi-portable chain saw.

1937-1939
- Worldwide production of saw chain reaches 40,000 to 50,000 feet per year.

1940-45
- World War II halts most power equipment production in favor of military hardware. Saw chain production averages about 1,500 feet per day.

1944
- Claude Poulan invents the chain saw bow guide from a piece of a truck fender to help German POWs cut wood in East Texas.

A photo of the author's collection of vintage chainsaws.

1946

- Claude Poulan founds Poulan Saw Company in Shreveport, Louisiana.

1948

- Stihl produces the first one-man chain saw, powered by a two-stroke engine.

1950-51

- Saw chain sales increase to approximately 2 million feet per year.

1951

- Lombard Governor Corporation starts selling a 16-inch, 27-pound saw.

1952

- Chain Saw Age publishes its first issue in August 1952 in Portland, Oregon. Major advertisers are Homelite, Oregon and McCullough.
- The first one-man chain saw produced by Dolmar was the 30-pound Model CP.

1952

- Ackley Manufacturing in Clackamas, Oregon, begins production of hydraulic chain saws.

1953

- Poulan completes new plant for production of an 11-model line.
- Strunk introduces a 3HP 19-inch one-man model.

1954

- U.S. farmers own one-quarter million chain saws.
- Stihl produces its first lightweight saw, 31 pounds.

1955

- U.S. chain saw exports total $8 million.
- Oregon Chain completes its new plant in Portland, Oregon, and introduces new $3/4$-inch pitch chipper chains 1AC, 3DAC and 3MAC.
- Stihl "Blitz" chain saw enters the U.S. market: 6 cubic inches, 26 pounds, lightest, most compact, best balanced gear reduced saw ever manufactured along with the direct drive model "Lightning" imported by Tull.
- Oregon introduces $7/16$-inch pitch Micro Bit chipper chain.

- U.S. chain saw exports total $11 million.
- U.S. Department of Commerce compiles production statistics of chain saws. Current estimate is $25 to $27 million annual chain saw sales.

1956

- Lancaster Pump, Lancaster, Pennsylvania, introduces Nifty chain saw for less than $150 with 3 HP engine with float-type carb and automatic cut-off switch.
- Trams, Chicago, Illinois, introduces new direct drive chain saw with 18 deluxe features, starting at $169.95.

1957

- U.S. chain saw exports total $9.5 million.
- Thirty chain saw manufacturers are located in the U.S. 400,000 chain saws are sold this year.
- McCullough nears 2 million feet per year chain production.

1957

- Shopmate offers the Suburban Logger, an electric unit convertible from $6^1/4$ inch circular to chain saw, expected to open a new market.

1958

- U.S. farmers own over one half million chain saws. There are 45 chain saw manufacturers worldwide, making over 200 different models.
- U.S. exports total $7.16 million. Total world annual production exceeds one half million for first time.

1959

- For the first time, more than one million chain saws are being used in the U.S.
- Homelite introduces 19 pound Buz at $153.50.
- Trams line's smallest is $2^1/2$ HP, 18 pounds, $119.50.

1959

- National Log Sawing Contest at Ely, Minnesota, holds a chain saw event won by Ken Brunner of Cook, Minnesota, using a Lombard Fury 81 with a Mighty Bite chain, clocking 6:01 minutes through 15-inch frozen green Norway Pine in -25°.

1960

- U.S. exports total $12.8 million; total world chain saw production is 607,000.

- Artist Mike Gildea, Manhattan Beach, California, uses chain saw for Tiki wood sculpture.
- Beaird-Poulan enters export market with large shipment to Australia. Counts over 1,000 U.S. dealers.

1961
- McCullough becomes the first manufacturer to advertise on network television.

1962
- U.S. chain saw exports total $12 million; consumers constitute less than five percent of chain saw market.
- McCullough becomes the first manufacturer to pass the one-million-saw mark.
- Kay Silvery wins a ladies event at a chain saw competition at the county fair in Plymouth, California.
- Ray Silvery, Kay's husband, wins the title at the First International Logging Championships held at World Fair, Seattle, Washington.
- General Chain Bar, Tigard Poland, Oregon, introduces roller-nose guide bars.

1963
- Gas-powered chain saws sold in the U.S. total 690,000 units; exports total $13.3 million.
- Solo introduces automatic chain lubrication.

1964
- U.S. chain saw exports total $18.7 million.

1966
- Non-professional consumers grow to 20 percent of the U.S. chain saw market, more than quadrupling in four years; one out of 20 American households owns a chain saw.
- Nine major East Coast logging shows feature chain saw contests this summer.
- Beaird-Poulan introduces Omark designed Safety Sharp self-sharpening system on lightweight production models.
- Stihl develops anti-vibration handles for chain saws.

1967
- Carlton introduces EZ Feed Chain and Sta-Sharp Chain.
- Stihl Chain Saws are used to power generators, cut ice for drinking water and operate winches at 60 degrees below zero on the Plaisted Polar Expedition, the first documented surface trip to North Pole. Saws provided by distributor Gene Alhborn, Wisconsin.

1970s–1980s
- Double raker, triple raker and preceding guard link saw chains are developed.
- Stihl introduces the Oilmatic self-lubricating chain.

A photo of the author's collection of vintage chainsaws.

1970

- K-S Industries, Santee, California, introduces the Kerf-Splitter Chain, the first major improvement in over 15 years.
- Oregon introduces sprocket nose bars, develops the first automatic chain tensioner.

1971

- Beaird-Poulan introduces the XXV consumer-size chain saw, which becomes a best seller.

1972

- The under-$140 market is five times as large as it was in 1970, growing from 50,000 units per year to 250,000.
- Jonsereds introduces an anti-kickback hand guard.
- Stihl introduces Oilomatic chain.

1973

- Over one million chain saws are sold in one year. More than 850,000 saws go to occasional users; the professional market consumes 110,000 saws; and commercial users absorb 80,000.
- Husqvarna's three-model line features hand guard breaks plus vibration and noise reduction without power loss.

1974

- Gas and electric chain saw sales exceed 3.5 million worldwide; 2.8 million gas-powered worldwide.
- Carlton introduces Ss Safety System saw chain and File-O-Plate.

1975

- Dolmar introduces the KMS4, the world's first Wankel rotary piston chain saw.
- Oregon introduces replaceable sprocket nose.
- Power Saw Manufacturers Association adds members, increases legislative efforts in Canada and U.S., drafts engineering standards and issues safety literature for manufacturers to include with new saw sales.

1976

- Domestic U.S.-made chain saw sales reach 1.7 million units.
- Sabre introduces anti-kickback AVS chain.

1977

- Domestic chain saw sales reach 2.5 million.

1978

- U.S. chain saw sales are 2.9 million units.
- Homelite sponsors the first Tournament of Kings invitational chain saw meet. Roy Booth Sr. wins first place.

1979

- Gas-powered U.S. chain saw sales are nearly 3 million; electrics, 8 million.
- Thor Power Tool of Aurara, Illinois, introduces the hydraulic chain saw.

1980

- Tight economic conditions and high energy prices push many homeowners to woodburning stoves, causing a jump in saw sales.

1981

- Gas-powered chain saw sales in the U.S. total 1.84 million units; electrics, just under one half million.
- Canadian Safety Standard requires chain brake on all gas-powered saws.
- National Equipment Servicing Dealer's Association forms in Pittsburgh, Pennsylvania.

1982

- New triple saw chain is proven to reduce kickback energy by levels up to 80 percent.

1982

- Approximately 18 million chain saws are currently in use in the U.S.
- U.S. Consumer Product Safety Commission announces its intention to develop mandatory chain saw safety standards.

1986

- The American National Standards Institute sets forth the minimum safety requirements for gasoline-powered chain saws.

Part Three:
Chainsaw Carving

CHAIN SAW SAFETY RULES

- Do not use a chain saw too big or too powerful for you to control. (See "Choosing a Team of Chain Saws" on page 95.)
- Do not rear handle throw start your chain saw.
- Only use chain saws with chain brakes. A chain brake will stop the chain from turning. This safety feature can prevent many injuries.
- Use anti-kick saw chain for the first five years.
- Never file rakers or guard links lower than the chain manufacturer's specifications.
- Be sure all nuts, bolts and screws are in place and tight—especially on the handles.
- Do not use a saw that is missing handle mount fasteners.
- Do plunge cuts and tip work only with reduced kickback tipped carving bars, with tips the size of a dime or a quarter.
- If you must plunge cut, start the cut with the rear of the bar lower than the center of the tip to the perpendicular and continue the cut in and down. Not in and up.

- Do not operate a chain saw if you are under the influence of any drug.
- Do not operate a chain saw if you are extremely fatigued for any reason, including a long drive, excessive lifting or other hard work, physical illness, mental stress, use of prescription or over-the-counter drugs, or alcohol.
- Be in good physical and mental health.
- Wear safety chaps, eye protection, ear protection, steel-toed boots and safety gloves.
- Constantly clean up debris from under foot.
- Be sure your project is firmly secured before you start cutting. Wood that is not on even ground and steady may move as you carve and cause you to lose control of the saw.
- Assume a good stance before each cut.
- Keep safe working distance between yourself and other living creatures.
- Do not work in an area where you may cause injury to others with flying debris. I use roped-off and netted-off areas for public demonstrations. My carving field is legally posted and is designated a dangerous work zone to protect curiosity seekers from harm and myself from legal action. The insurance company that carries my liability policy has reduced my insurance costs dramatically because of this signage.
- Many of the injuries incurred by chainsaws are caused by lack of attention to the location of the bar and chain of a running saw. Either shut of your saw or use the chain brake while your eyes and your other hand are attending other quick chores. For example, do not continue to hold a running saw with your left hand while pulling out a small wedge cut with your right hand.

Plunge Cutting and Bar Tip Kickback

I am not recommending plunge cutting here. I am recommending safety hints for those who do plunge cut. There are two very important precautions you can take to reduce bar tip kickback.

First, never file or let any one else file your saw chain rakers lower than the manufacturer's specifications. When the rakers have been lowered too far, several unpleasant results may occur. 1) The chain will be extremely susceptible to kickback. 2) The cutters will be too aggressive and may jump, chatter, stick in the wood and stop the chain from turning. 3) When used on extremely dry hard wood, the chain may break.

Second, the potential for kickback increases when you use a technique called plunge cutting. Plunge cutting is when you push the saw blade into the wood. It can be dangerous and it is not a technique I recommend for the novice chain saw carver. If you must plunge cut, start with the rear of the bar lower than the center of the tip and continue the cut in and down—not in and up.

The drawings above show the reduced kickback radius of a carving bar (left) and a standard utility bar (right). Kickback zones are marked in black.

To plunge cut, start with the rear of the bar lower than the center of the tip and continue the cut in and down, not in and up.

Safety Gear

Safety gear is as necessary to chain saw carvers as the chain saw itself. If you don't have a chain saw, you can't carve. If you don't have the proper safety gear, don't carve. The following is a sampling of the safety gear that is available to chain saw carvers.

- Eye protection is a definite must. Your eye protection choice will depend on your personal preference. Safety glasses, goggles and face screens are all readily available. I prefer glasses first and face screens second.
- Ear protection is no longer a burden with modern ear

muffs. These muffs are designed to deaden and filter out damaging sounds. They also help you cut down on outside stress factors, leaving your mind free to concentrate on your work.

- From the standpoint of a chain saw carver, chain saw safety chaps are the best invention since the tiltable carburetor. These chaps not only give the carver protection from possible cuts, but also protect his legs from gas, oil and dirt. This in turn eliminates discomfort and fatigue, allowing better concentration. Last, but not least, chaps come off in seconds and you can walk or drive around in comfort and without looking nearly as grungy as you would if you had not worn chaps.
- Steel-toe boots offer protection from dropped chain saws and falling pieces of wood.
- Chain saw safety gloves are another good choice. They offer solid protection for your hands and are available at better chain saw shops.

Work Space

If you're using a gas saw, the best place to work is outside. Again, make sure that no one—animal or human—is within 20 ft. of your work space. Use rope or netting to create a safety zone.

Electric saws can be used indoors. Again, make sure you have ample room to work and that people and pets are out of danger's way.

Before you begin a chain saw carving project, check with your local government to make sure they don't have any zoning laws or noise ordinances that would affect your working space and time. Contacting the neighbors about your endeavor is common courtesy and might save you some heated debates later on.

CHOOSING A TEAM OF SAWS

Choosing a team of chain saws for carving might be mind boggling to some. A single manufacturer may produce a dozen or more models for you to consider. A few companies produce several saws with no real range of power difference. The bottom line is that you need to research a saw carefully and to thoroughly understand the logistics of the project you are planning before choosing a saw.

When purchasing a chain saw for carving, you should attempt to match the saw's weight and speed ratio with a number of different factors. Consider the following: your physical condition and capabilities; your hand/eye coordination; your brain's ability to study and maintain the correct form, line and detail of the subject you are planning to carve; and your experience and comfort level operating a chain saw. If you rate yourself high in these areas, you should be able to handle a more powerful saw than someone who rates himself low in these areas.

Taking all these factors into consideration, I have developed a chart of the four basic saw sizes and accompanying

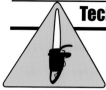

TechTip

The most comfortable working height for making the perpendicular cuts and the angular cuts is about knee level. The most comfortable height at which to make horizontal or ripping cuts is from elbow level to slightly below the belt.

bars and chains that I use in heavy production every day. (See the chart below.) These selections are based on over 15 years of personal chain saw carving experience. Those saws are then keyed to the users as they are described below. Find your level of experience, then choose a team of chain saws.

Use the chart below to help you choose a team of chain saws for your project. First, decide on your level of experience, then match the description to the saws.

   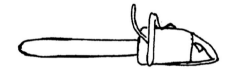

A.	B.	C.	D.
2.1 Cubic Inches	3.1 Cubic Inches	4.1 Cubic Inches	5.7 Cubic Inches
35 CC	50 CC	66 CC	93+ CC
Dime Tip 12 in. Carving Bar	18 in. Sprocket Nose	24 in. Sprocket Nose	(1) 30 in. Sprocket Nose Bar
$1/4$ Pitch	$3/8$" Pitch LP or 325 Pitch	$3/8$ Pitch Standard	(1) 50 in. Sprocket Nose Bar
			$3/8$" or 404 Pitch

BEGINNER chain saw carver with NO CHAIN SAW EXPERIENCE. Choose one saw from category A and one saw from category B with guard links on all chains.

BEGINNER chain saw carver with OVER 1,000 HOURS of chain saw operating experience. Choose one saw from category A; one from category B; and one from category C with guard links on saws A and B.

EXPERIENCED chain saw carver with OVER 5 YEARS of chain saw carving experience, in good physical and mental health. Choose two saws from category A; one from category B with a 14 in. carving bar; two from category C (one with an 18 in. carving bar); and one from category D.

EXPERIENCED chain saw carver EARNING OVER $55,000 A YEAR and hoping to double that figure without doubling work time or human energy. Choose five saws from category A; two saws from category B with 14 in. quarter tips; three from category C (one with a 14 in. quarter tip and one with an 18 in. quarter tip; and two from category D (one with a 30 in. bar and one with a 50 in. bar).

CHAINSAW MILLING

Some chain saw carvers use 2-by-6 boards glued and clamped together to make large flat panels on which to carve relief projects. I prefer to use this method only when I'm working on doors and large wall murals.

For most of my projects, I use a chainsaw mill to cut my own wood. With this set-up, my chain saw is combined with other hardware to create a miniature mill. It is an ideal way to avoid high costs of milled wood, mill logs where they fall, mill crotched or extremely bowed logs for specialized projects, and mill wide logs and burls. I can also mill angled "slices" of wood for relief and silhouetted projects with ease.

I mill pine and catalpa about 3 in. thick; black walnut and butternut about 1 3/4 in. thick. The logs I mill are usually 22 in. to 35 in. diameter. I mill them at whatever length they are when they arrive at my work site.

Among the most obvious reasons why a carver might want to mill his or her own project wood are:

- You most likely cannot buy what you want or need at the local lumber yard or saw mill.
- There is no middle-man 50-percent mark up on wood
- You can mill logs where they fall, with no need for heavy skidding, loading and transporting equipment.
- You can mill logs at the angle you desire.
- You can mill extremely curved or bowed logs for specialized projects. You can mill logs as long and as thick as you desire.

- You can mill wider logs than 90 percent of the commercial saw mills in the US. You can also mill crotches, stump bases and large burs.
- You can take advantage of yard tree removal and of ornamental shade tree removal for select woods, such as catalpa, butternut, walnut and fruit trees.
- On occasions when you are doing large carvings with logs over 25" in diameter and over six feet tall, the carvings' designs may require the front and the back of the log to be removed. If you mill this excess wood off the log rather than just rip it off as waste, your extra time spent in milling may help you earn an additional few thousand dollars from your log.
- No commercial saw mill will accept yard trees, as they may contain foreign material, which will destroy expensive equipment and perhaps cause injury to mill workers. With a horizontal chainsaw mill operated below eye level, the most you can loose is a saw chain and some time.

After all the time invested in milling, stacking, drying, end grain sealing, it is extremely disheartening to find that the wood you assumed was well vented and drying was actually molding and rotting. To prevent this, restack your wood every two or three months using new dry spacers or stickers, even if you have it in a dry building. Do this for at least the first two years. If you keep the wood longer than two years, change every six months or so thereafter.

Finished Lumber Guide

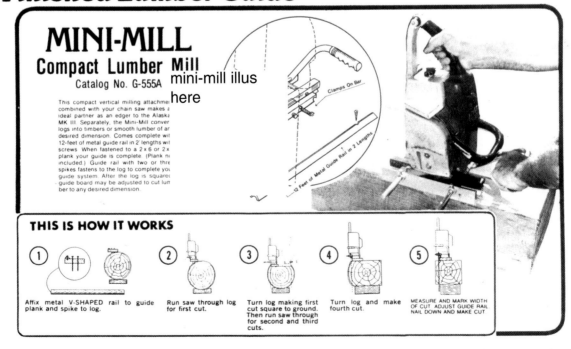

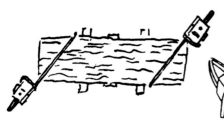

Drawing A—Both ends of the log were cut on the same angle. A tape measure was used to mark for the second cut to improved the possibility that both ends will be somewhat uniform.

To elevate one end of the log, roll it up onto balancing or pivot log by using scrap wood or smaller logs, bracing as you go.

If you cannot manually tip up the project log after it has been rolled up onto a pivot log, even using peavies, cant hook and leverage poles, and you do not own any hydraulic lifting equipment (e.g., power tail gate; forklift; bucket lift), you can sometimes use a large bumper jack. Elevate the log in stages and brace underneath as you raise it. Top surface does not have to be perfectly level as long as there is clearance space.

I carved these Wolves on an angular slab of catalpa; dimensions are approximately 44 in. by 24 in. by 3 in. Both were chainsaw milled from a single seven-foot angular-cut log. About 21 such slabs can be milled from one seven-foot log. These short slabs can be stacked and stored in a relative small space (compared to most chain saw carving project woods) and turned into profitable inventory during the harshest months of the winter.

Drawing B—Ten inch waste block is removed before milling to allow space to remove saw bar and mill after each cut.

Drawing C—Common use of mill to produce project wood. For Alaskan milled cuts, you will need two plastic wedges to be placed behind the bar in the kerf on each side just before the end of the milling cut is severed. This will prevent the slab from pinching the chain after the cut is completed.

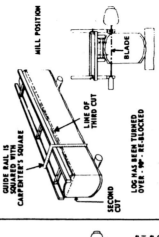

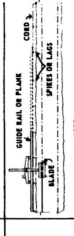

PREPARING GUIDE RAIL OR GUIDE PLANK

An accurate dependable guide system is absolutely necessary before attempting to operate your "ALASKAN"® Granberg Industries has perfected a steel spreader-bracket, anchoring spikes, which when spaced and bolted in position every four to five feet between two straight 2" x 4"'s make the ideal guide rail for your chainsaw mill. If you have not as yet obtained these brackets, a guide may be fashioned from a good straight 2" x 12" plank with 2" x 2's or angle irons securely fastened to the plank edges to form a saddle rest when plank is placed on the log in preparation for the first cut.

GUIDE RAIL

GUIDE PLANKS

2" x 2" LBR.

ANGLE IRON

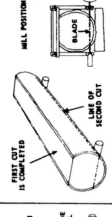

GUIDE RAIL IS POSITIONED

MILL POSITION

GUIDE RAIL

BLADE

LINE OF FIRST CUT

SETTING UP FOR THE FIRST CUT

Place the guide rail or plank on the log and secure. The guide rail must project at least six inches beyond the ends of the log so that the saw will leave the cut level and evenly. This basic or first cut determines the accuracy of all later cuts, so make sure it will be true and level and that the greatest amount of lumber will be produced from the log.

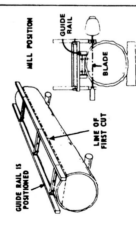

FIRST CUT IS COMPLETED

LINE OF SECOND CUT

MILL POSITION

BLADE

MAKING READY FOR THE SECOND CUT

Remove the guide rail and slab as the mill rails will now slide on the level surface of the first cut while making the parallel second cut. Lower the blade, using the thickness gauge to the lumber dimension desired. If, for instance, you are planning to make planking—the slab to be taken from the bottom of the log will be approximately the same size as the slab from the first cut. Wedge this cut open as the saw comes out of cut to prevent the saw bar from pinching.

CENTER ON-OFF GUIDE BAR IN MIDDLE OF LOG TO LEAD SAW IN AND OUT OF CUT

GUIDE RAIL IS SQUARED WITH CARPENTER'S SQUARE

MILL POSITION

BLADE

LINE OF THIRD CUT

SECOND CUT

LOG HAS BEEN TURNED OVER - 90° - RE-BLOCKED

PREPARING TO MAKE THE THIRD CUT

Now rotate the log 90° and brace the log firmly. Replace and fasten the guide rail. Use a carpenter's square to insure that the third slabbing cut will be at right angles to the faces of the first and second cuts.

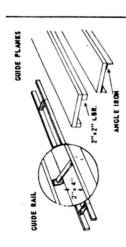

THIRD CUT COMPLETED

MILL POSITION FOR TOP CUT IN THIS SERIES

BLADE

LINES OF SUBSEQUENT CUTS-VARIOUS THICKNESSES

ON-OFF GUIDE BAR GIVES A LEVEL START (FINISH) IN & OUT OF LOG

CENTER ON-OFF GUIDE BAR ON CANT

READY TO CONVERT CANT INTO LUMBER

You are now ready to convert the cant into lumber. Remove the slab and guide rail. Determine the thickness of the planks or boards. to be produced and set the gauge to the correct thickness. Remember that the mill slides on the level surface of each previous cut so take care that the on-off guide bar is centered on the cant to insure the saw enters and leaves the cut evenly.

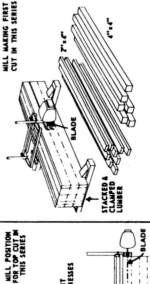

MILL MAKING FIRST CUT IN THIS SERIES

BLADE

STACKED & CLAMPED LUMBER

2" x 6"

4" x 4"

MAKING DIMENSION LUMBER FROM SAWN PLANKS

When you desire to make dimension lumber; gather the saw planks as shown and clamp firmly. Now adjust the thickness gauge as required so as to cut 2" x 2"'s, 2" x 6"'s or 2" x 12"'s as an example. Keep in mind that if various sizes are planned to be taken from the same log, such as 4" x 4"'s, 6" x 6"'s, 4" x 8"'s, etc, the various dimensions needed must be allowed for when making the previous cuts. See Step Five.

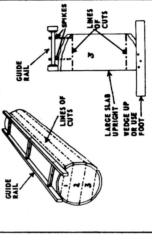

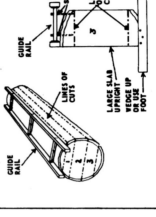

GUIDE RAIL

SPIKES

LINES OF CUTS

GUIDE RAIL

LINES OF CUTS

LARGE SLAB UPRIGHT

WEDGE UP OR USE FOOT

TIMBERS–CANTS–BEAMS–ETC., FROM LARGE LOGS

To split larger logs into two or more sections, proceed as in Step Two. The size of these heavy, pieces are controlled by the setting of the thickness frame. The guide rail is used in the same manner as previously described (Step Two). The cuts may require wedging open due to heavy weight.

GUIDE RAIL OR PLANK

CORD

GUIDE RAIL

LINES OF TOP & BOTTOM CUTS

CORD

SPIKES OR LAGS

LOG TURNED

BLADE

SPIKES OR LAGS

TAUT CORD

STEPS TAKEN IN THE MAKING OF PREMIUM LENGTH BEAMS

When cutting extra long or premium beams, use two guide rails or planks for the initial cut. Before placing the guide rails, stretch a heavy cord from one end of the log to the other. Drive spikes or lags to the height of the cord as a means of keeping the guide rails true and level. When the mill has passed beyond the first guide rail, remove the guide rail. Proceed in this step and repeat process for the entire length of the log. When using one guide rail, raise the mill and slide the guide rail ahead along the heads of the logs or spikes.

776-L10

Granberg Industries, Inc.   200 South Garrard Blvd., Richmond, CA 94804

Line Drawing

Over the past several years many chain saw carvers who own and operate a sales shop have called and written, wanting to know what they can make for $30 or less. They have noticed that many of the people coming in their door want to buy something, but are limited by one or all of the following factors: limited space in their home or yard, too heavy to transport, or short on finances. Of course, some customers will buy line drawings simply because they like the work.

Whatever you call them—Chain Saw Timber Doodles, line drawings, scratch boards, hen scratchings or chain saw chip carvings—they are also perfect for beginning chain saw carvers. Line drawings can be made from almost any scrap lumber and they will help you improve your texturing and drawing skills.

There are two basic approaches to creating chain saw line drawings, both of which require using the tip of a carving bar. One is to cut a straight or curved line of uniform depth and width. The other is to apply the tip of the carving bar to the wood using varying amounts of restraint or pressure with an across-and-down movement.

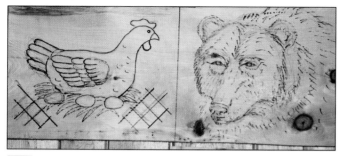

1 Make up enough drawings to keep you busy for a few hours. If you're a beginning chain saw carver, you'll want to start with a pattern that's simplistic and big, such as this chicken. More advanced chain saw carvers may wish to challenge themselves with smaller, more intricate designs.

2 To make a v-cut of a uniform depth and at a consistent angle, you must angle the tip of the carving bar according to the curve of the line. Curves that bow upward should be cut from below; those that bow downward should be cut from above.

3 In the same manner, lines that curve to the left should be cut from the right; lines that curve to the right should be cut from the left.

4 Line drawings can also be made with cuts of varying depths and different angles. The variations make it possible to express fine, medium and bold textures and lines.

5 Notice the varying depths and lengths of saw chain scratches on the bear's muzzle. Deeper cuts are achieved by applying more pressure as you apply the side of the bar tip to the wood; shallow cuts require very little pressure.

6 This log cabin scene combines the two techniques. I use cuts of varying depth and angles for the branches of the pine tree.

7 I create the lines of the cabin with cuts of the same depth and angle. Gas saws run at variable speeds, and the speed of the saw can be increased or decreased as you carve.

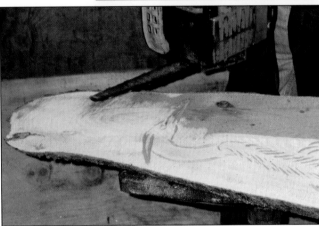

8 Line drawings look great in color. First, coat all the lines with spray paint. After the paint dries, remove any excess paint by planing the surface with the chain saw. Hold the saw with the long flat upward edge of the cutting system touching the wood at about an 11-degree angle. With a smooth gliding motion, move the saw to your left, or toward the belly of the saw. Maintain an even pressure on the working long edge of the bar.

9 The remainder of the color, stain and sealer is sprayed on or brushed on after the lines have been colored and the surface has been planed.

Shallow Relief

Chain saws can also be used to make shallow relief carvings. Unlike line drawings, where an image is drawn into the wood, the detail in shallow relief carvings is raised above the background.

Find a good book on painting duck decoys. I use the one by Anthony Hillman published by Dover. This is a stapled book that is easily disassembled for shop use.

Draw out the patterns on suitable cardboard. Cut out patterns and use a sharp knife to indicate critical reference points on the pattern, such as eyes, feather rows, inner bill lines, and so on.

Locate or make a suitable working table to draw and paint on. I like using two steel 50 gallon drums to support the planks. The drums can also double as a container for shop scraps and fire wood.

1 For this project, I'll be carving ducks. I use 2x10 planks of either spruce, pine or fir. Be sure the planks are not warped, cupped or cracked and do not have ring checks, rotten areas or dry knots.

2 I will be creating a number of duck carvings for sale, so to make them all look similar, I use patterns. Patterns expedite drawing time and increase uniformity. I trace the patterns onto cardboard and use a sharp knife to trace over any important reference lines, such as eyes, feather rows and inner bill lines. I then cut out the patterns and the marked areas, secure the patterns on the wood with push pins, and trace them with a marker.

4 The first step in removing the background is to make an oblique cut. This cut also allows me to see the tip of the bar when I make the horizontal cuts in the next step.

5 I make a flat, horizontal cut to remove the remainder of the background. Next, I will round the edges by holding the saw at a sharp angle. The cuts to define the feathers are made at a lower angle. I clean up the eyes using a small gouge.

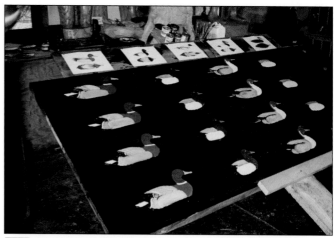

6 I use an acetylene torch to darken the background of the carving and raise the wood grain. Once the surface is evenly charred, I use a stiff-bristled brush—not a wire brush—to remove the soot and burned wood. An air hose is used for a final dusting. I clean up the eyes with a small gouge

After the planks are clean, I apply a coat of polyurethane to the background of the carving. Be careful not to get urethane on the decoys. It will cause the paint to have a plastic or enamel look.

7 All the decoys to be painted are laid out along with the color plates for those ducks. I paint all of the areas that are the same color at one time. This helps to maintain a consistent look among the pieces and makes painting move along much faster.

Use a perpendicular cut to outline the drawing.

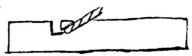

Use an oblique cut to begin removing the background.

Use a flat, horizontal cut to remove the rest of the background.

Round off the edges with an angled cut.

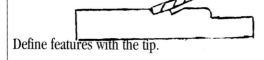

Define features with the tip.

Shallow relief cabinet doors, 41 in. by 19 in., 37 in. by 17 1/2 in.
By Hal MacIntosh, Northern Catskill Mountains, NY, 1999.

Shallow relief mural, by Hal MacIntosh, 1981. Billbos Restaurant, Durango, Colorado.

Shallow relief exterior doors in southwest Colorado. By Hal MacIntosh.

Pierced Relief

Some chain saw carvers use 2-by-6 glued and clamped wood to make up suitable large flat panels. I only use this method for doors and large wall murals. I use chain saw milled slabs. I mill pine and catalpa, 3" thick; black walnut and butternut about 1 3/4". The logs I mill are usually 22" to 35" in diameter and milled at whatever length they are when they arrive at my work site. The bark on white pine slabs must be removed or treated before the bore season.

To begin the drying process, I stack the milled slabs, using spacers or stickers between each piece. I cap each stack with the outside half round. If I have time, I treat the ends with an end grain wood sealer, such as Anchor Seal. This prevents end check-ing. After the slabs have been exposed to the outdoor elements, I move them indoors to complete the drying process.

The drying period in the more arid parts of the country are not the same as in the humid regions. The length of time to dry this wood will depend on many factors. Of course, slabs milled from a standing dead tree are going to dry faster than ones cut from a green log of the same species in the same region.

Design and Subject

I collect and study wildlife magazines and videos to stimulate ideas. Perhaps the best ideas are created on a doodle pad at the kitchen table.

1 Pencil lines and cross-hatches show areas to be relieved or removed.
Use a pencil to draw in the main subject, background and frame. If erasing becomes difficult, use a power sander or skim off the marks with the top back side of your saw bar running nearly parallel with the slab. Use a bold, black ink marker or logger's crayon to sharply define the final lines. Use a different color to make cross-hatched marks to indicate the areas to be pierce-cut. A third color indicates the area to be relieved.

2 Blackened areas show areas that will be pierced and removed.
Using a chain saw equipped with your best dime tip carving bar, make perpendicular cuts about 3/4 in. deep to better define the border lines. Next, working inside these lines, plunge cut completely through the carving in straight lines to remove the bulk of the wood. Next, cut out the smaller wedge-shaped pieces that indicate the tops of the trees and the edges of the outer feathers.

3 Blackened areas show areas that will be relieved the deepest.
The blackened area of the far wing is removed by making a perpendicular cut down the front line of the near wing and tapered to the end on the front part of the near wing to the next. The next cut is made from the side, slicing off the appropriate area, as deep as the near wing kerf in the rear and tapering to a desired ending point. The trees in the background may be started with the same method. However, the frame and the main subject will prevent you from merely slicing off unwanted wood. The remainder of the tree can be removed by gliding the bottom of the bar tip back and forth over the high spots. Texturing of the trees at this time will also relieve them deeper.

This Eagle carving shows a large bass upside down and backward after an awkward catch and near loss. If I were making a carving to be reproduced in plastic for chain store sales, I would use a trout right side up and forward.

A very important aspect in choosing which design or subject to do at a given time may be greatly influenced by your financial needs. Then you have to choose a design that you believe will sell well.

Patterns

I personally do not make patterns for first-time relief carvings. On the walls of my shop I maintain what I call a catalog display inventory. These carvings are not for sale. If I receive several custom orders for a given carving, then I make a pattern from the original on heavy corrugated cardboard. After I fill the orders, I frequently produce three or four extra copies for sales room inventory.

Setting Up Project Wood

A little extra time and effort in setting up the project wood will be recovered in the first hour of work. The most comfortable and safest working height is between knee level and breast heights. This may be achieved by using large round blocks of various thickness cut flat on one side. I use 12-by-12 pine blocks about three feet long, stacked in varying configurations, allowing for the work area surface to be adjusted as needed.

Regardless of the method you use to make a temporary work bench, be sure your bar tip on the piercing maneuver does not strike anything behind the back surface of the carving.

Texturing

Anyone not familiar with chain saw carving might be surprised to learn that shaping, smoothing and texturing can often be accomplished with one stroke or sweep. The easiest way I know of to explain texturing is to think of the long-hand writing exercises you did in grade school. Practice up and down, as well as across. Practice making rows of connecting V's and half C's. If you look at the textures on drawing B you will notice that the body feathers were done with a sloppy back and forth V type scribble motion. The half C lines to texture the wing feathers are done two ways. Some are drawn in with the edge of the tip. Others are suggested less vividly with gliding, skipping motions.

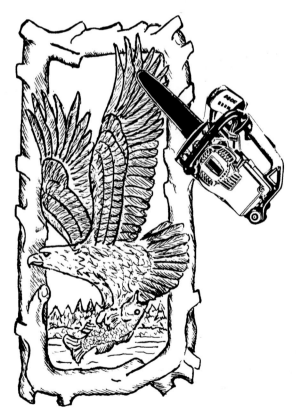

| 4 | Blackened areas show the second deepest relief cuts.

Remove the wood from these areas in the same manner as in Step 2.

| 5 | Blackened areas show the shallowest relief cuts.

Remove the wood from these areas in the same manner as in Step 2.

| 6 | Shallow cuts add texture.

Draw in the separation of the remaining wing and tail feathers and any other textured details necessary to complete the carving.

The pierced areas of the carving have been cut away and the frame has been cut to shape.

The different levels of the carving have been relieved.

The finished eagle carving by Hal MacIntosh.

Care for Relief Carving Projects

1. Do not work in direct sunlight.

2. Once you have started your carving, do not leave it in extreme heat, dryness, or moisture.

3. Keep both your unused relief project wood and your unfinished carving laying on a flat surface when not being worked.

4. After you have completed the carving, seal all edges and the front. I use urethane and lacquers. I have in the past, used end grain wax.

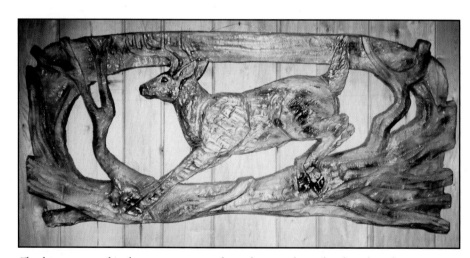

The deer was carved in the same manner as the eagle. It was burned and urethaned, 57 in. by 25 in. by 3 in. By Hal MacIntosh.

Pierced Relief

A second pierced relief carving project will give you a closer look at the carving in progress. If you are a beginning chain saw carver, you might be surprised to learn that the shaping, smoothing and texturing of many carvings can often be accomplished with one stroke. The easiest way I know to tell you to practice these texturing methods is to think of the long-hand writing exercises you did in grade school—except don't stay within two horizontal lines; practice up and down as well as across. Try making rows of connecting V's and half C's as a practice exercise before you tackle this project.

Pierced relief designs ready for the author to start carving.

1 The slab of dried catalpa cut at an angle is ready for carving. The wolf carving on the right was completed with the same methods.

2 I use two utility benches and an 8 x 8 as a work surface. Nails driven into the benches at the base of the carving keep it from skidding. When I work on the piercing part of this carving, I'll spread the benches apart and lay the wood flat on the two benches so that the saw blade can pass completely through the carving without hitting any obstructions.

3 I hold the saw bar tip perpendicular to the surface to define the symmetrical shape of the spear head.

4 Here, the trailing edge of the almost flatly placed saw bar is being skimmed across the frame's surface to remove some of the deepest chain marks and to achieve uniformity in the thickness of the frame.

5 | Again, operating the saw while it is held nearly flat will plane out saw marks and textures on the subject's neck and chest.

6 | I use one stroke to plane and shape the forehead, as well as define and emphasize the hairline.

7 | I carve out the center of the horse's ear and texture it at the same time.

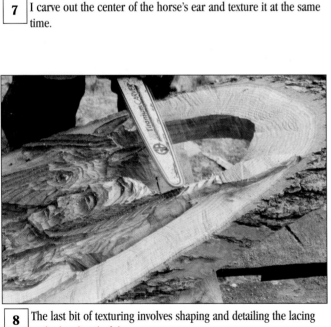

8 | The last bit of texturing involves shaping and detailing the lacing at the head end of the spear.

The finished pierced relief carving by Hal MacIntosh.

Silhouette Relief

Half round mill scraps were used to carve these stylized wildlife creatures.

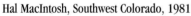

Hal MacIntosh, Southwest Colorado, 1981

Step Cutting

Step cuts are the first step in creating an in-the-round sculpture. I have included two step cut projects in this section. The Craft-Style Bear Head is a simple project that requires only basic cuts to complete. Yet the finished project is the perfect testament to a novice chain saw carver's growing talent. You can then texture the bear with the techniques you learned in the previous lessons. The Log Cabin with Trees is a more advanced project. It requires numerous step cuts and plunge cuts. Make sure you are comfortable with your saw and plunge cuts before you tackle this second project.

Craft Style Bear

Black Bear

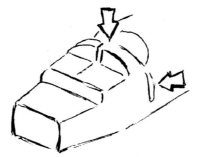

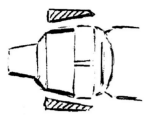

There are several methods you can use to round and shape your bear head after you complete the step cuts. Where possible I prefer to stand in front of the carving to shape the nose, head, chin and ears. The top inside trailing edge of the bar can be used to "skim down" the edges more gradually. You can also round and shape the bear as you put in the hair texture. In the photo of the two craft bear heads, I had to use a scaffold. While carving the head nearest the camera, I could position my body and saw almost any way I wanted. The far side of the outer bear, however, was even with the outer railing. I had to carve this area of the bear from above and below.

Three-Dimensional Step Cutting

There are numerous reasons this project of a log cabin with trees is a good exercise for experienced novice chain saw carvers. Unlike human or wildlife studies, this project does not require that all aspects of the piece be in exact proportion and relationship to one another. You must however, keep in your minds' eye at all times during the step cuts, the relationship and alignment of the tree's trunk and the front and back walls of the cabin. Also be aware of the top tip of the trees' alignment with the trunks.

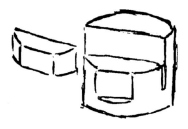
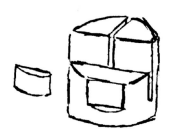
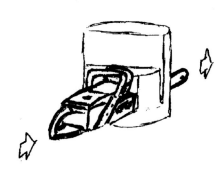
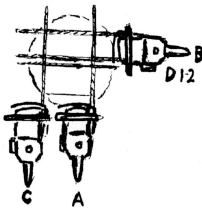

1. Make the first cut just off-center. About 55–60 percent of one side will be used for the trees. The smaller side will be used for the cabin. The cut shown in the illustration shows the split for the two areas.

2. Next, make a vertical cut. This cut determines the outer edge of the cabin. Make a horizontal cut to remove the piece. The horizontal cut determines the final maximum thickness of the base.

3. Make a vertical cut where the top of the chimney is located.

4. Make a center cut to divide the two trees.

5. Make the first plunge cut (A) at a right angle to the base. This marks the outside edge of the cabin. The width of your utility bar determines the height of the cabin walls and height of the unbranched tree trunks.

6. The second plunge cut (B) removes the wood on the outer edge of the tree trunks at the far side of the cabin. The third plunge cut (C) determines the outer edge of the cabin's fireplace and approximate back of the rear tree trunk. The fourth plunge cut (D) determines the outer edge of the tree nearest to the cabin. At least one or two more plunge cuts should be made between this cut and the tree and cabin dividing cut.

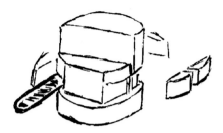

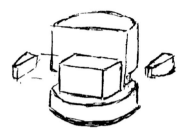

7. Follow each vertical plunge cut with two horizontal cuts—one top and one bottom—to remove the blocks of wood.

8. Use an up-cut to remove the protruding blocks from the cabin peak and the fireplace.

9. Slab off the outside edges of the trees, as shown in the drawing.

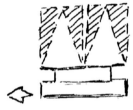

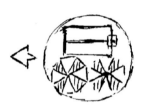

10. Cut off the other two sides of each tree to form an elongated pyramid.

11. Make series of short plunge cuts to open the space between the two tree trunks.

12. Shave off the square edges of the pyramids to achieve an octagon-like cone effect. Then round off the sharp edges to form cones.

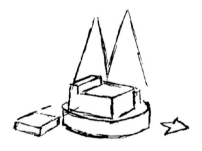

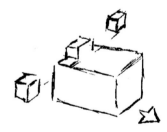

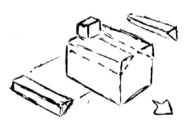

13. This step removes the block of wood that determines the maximum height of the roof's peak and the height the chimney will be above the peak.

14. Removing the blocks that form the chimney may require a series of down-cuts and side-grinding with the tip of your bar. Side-grinding is simply fanning the running saw back and forth close to your carving to remove very small amounts of wood.

15. Use a detailing saw with a dime or quarter tip carving bar for the rest of the carving. To form the peak, I shave off the roof's angles by cutting down and out from the top with the tip of the bar nearly touching the chimney. After I cut down past the chimney, I push the bar forward, plunge cutting off the pitch on the side of the chimney.

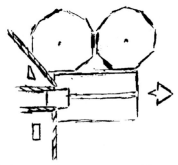

16. The protruding rear portion of the stone work on the chimney can be achieved by making a shallow cut one-third to one-half the thickness of the chimney. Then make a right angle cut to that cut forming the back edge of the cabin and the stone work.

17. To create the boughs and needle texture of the pine trees, start at the peak of the tree and make a shallow, short, angular cut down and forward. Flick the tip of your bar out and away from the tree instead of just removing it downward. This little outward flick creates a ragged bough effect on the lower edge.

18. A second cut is necessary to form the bough. Move slightly to the left and make an angular up-cut.

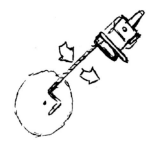

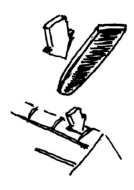

19. The needles and uneven texture of the boughs of the tree are achieved by holding the rear handle downward and sweeping the top, curved portion of the bar against the area being textured.

20. Repeat these steps for each cluster of branches. Remember, you do not want a cross-hatched, pineapple-like effect.

21. Next, round off and shape the tree trunks and clean up the ground. This clean-up can be achieved by merely fanning your bar from side to side in the upright position or up and down in the prone position.

22. Check the cabin for squareness. If the cabin is out-of-square, make the necessary alterations. Reshape and center the pitch of the cabin and smooth out any nicks that might occurred while working on the trees.

23. To achieve the downward edge of the rows indicating the shingles or shakes, hold the saw at a slight angle to the long, top edge of the roof and make a shallow up-cut. The width of the first row of shingles will determine the width of the remaining rows.

24. To create the division line between each individual shingle, lay the cutting edge of the bar tip where you want the line to be and cut the single line. Do the entire top row. The dividing lines on each adjoining row will alternate with the row immediately above it.

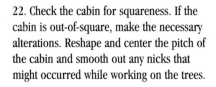

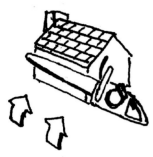

25. Make the eaves and the indents for the door and windows by gently fanning the tip of the bar from side to side in the desired area. The lines separating each row of logs on the long sides of the cabin are achieved in the same manner as the lines that defined the shingles. The one major difference is to reduce the bar angle to achieve a more perpendicular cut to the side of the cabin. The lines that detail the stone work on the chimney are the most lightly scribed lines on the carving.

Make a pressure-relief cut between the cabin and the trees. The cut should extend from the edge of the base to the center, from the top clear to the bottom. This kerf will prevent the piece from cracking in an unacceptable direction.

Turn the carving upside down and clean up the bottom of the tree foliage. Do this in several different positions if necessary. Set the carving up-right and cut the bark off the base to prevent insect damage.

Because these carvings go so quickly once you have mastered the techniques, I often create a number of them at one time. These finished pieces are ready to be burned or painted.

Step Cutting a Life-sized Heron

Of all the step cut chain saw carving designs I have used in 45-minute chain saw carving competitions over the years, this stylized heron is the easiest and fastest.

Drawing A: The first cut is made to the left of center to achieve a narrow side. The second cut removes the wood on the opposite side of the first cut. This cut is much wider to allow for the bracing cattails or reeds at the side of the heron. The third cut removes the wood to the outside of the outer leg.

Plunge cuts are made to clear out the spaces between the legs. The first plunge cut clears the space between the inside of the outer leg and the open space between the two legs. The second plunge cut indicates the space between the reeds and the outer side of the inside leg. The third and fourth plunge cuts continue to clear out the space between the two legs. Be careful when making the first, third and fourth plunge cuts not to raise the bar too high and remove the wood for the tail.

Drawing B: After completing the cuts in Drawing A, a flat surface is left on which to draw out the head and neck. If you need guidelines, use a marker; more confident carvers can make guidelines with the tips of their chain saws. Because I am so familiar with this pattern, I often work with no guidelines other than the ones in my mind's eye. As you work, be sure to leave enough wood for the supporting reeds.

Drawing C: This drawing shows the opposite side of the carving from Drawing B. The dotted lines indicate the wood

to be removed from the side view. Use a detailing saw with a dime or quarter tip bar for the rest of this work.

Drawing D: The completed sculpture.

There are literally dozens upon dozens of designs of either standing or flying great blue herons you can carve, stylized or realistic.

Drawing E: Once you study this design you can see that using most of the same or similar step cuts shown in drawings A and B, you will be able to rapidly achieve roughing out this project. Drawing E is the proportionately and anatomically correct drawing of a great blue heron in this section.

Drawing F: This is merely a somewhat more realistic version of Drawing D.

Drawings G, H, I and J: These designs all show the bill and/or head or neck tucked in. Some carvers that do not trust their knowledge of wood characteristics or strength will prefer to use this type of design at first.

Drawing H: This may seem to be an impossible position for any bird, however, both the long neck herons and egrets can fold and twist their necks any way they want.

One winter high up in the Colorado Rockies where almost all waterways were frozen over and covered with snow, I came across a small open spot in the rapids of a nar-

row creek. A great blue heron stood on one leg in this open water, his head and bill were tucked so far in that he looked like a football balanced on a twig.

Drawings K and L: Both of these drawings show wading stalking birds.

Drawing M: This drawing is taken from a greatly stylized dual bird composition I used in a six-hour competition I did in the mid -1980s.

Before You Begin: Draw a line on top of the log left of the heart as you stand in front of the carving. Make a second parallel line about two inches to the left of that line in proportion to the diameter of and length of the log and the desired size of the completed project.

| 1 | The first cut removes the block to the far left side of the head and neck and starts to expose the left shoulder. |

| 2 | Here I am using a 3.0 cu. in. model 2050 Jonsered turbo, with 325 pitch full chisel chain. The bar is a standard sprocket nose utility bar. Bigger saws above 4.5 cu. in. are not necessary for small jobs such as this (with the exception of speed cutting competitions.) |

| 3 | Left side view of completed first cut. There are two ways to accomplish this cut. One is to cut down straight and taper the cut out at the shoulder. An older used bar and chain with the lower portion of the bar rails worn to both sides will allow for ease in curved cutting. A new bar with a uniform square shoulder and base in conjunction with fresh squared drive links on the new chain will make curved cutting less efficient. If a new bar and chain is being used make a straight down cut to the top of the shoulders then make a second up from the bottom following your marks to meet with your previously made down cut. |

| 4 | This photo shows the front view of the project. The right side, or flora side, is marked on the top of the log slightly to the left of the heart, or about two inches left of center. |

5 | A view of the project with the first two step cuts completed.

6 | In this view, notice how ragged the top of the far right cut is. This was caused by the rakers on the saw chain being filed too low for this dry hardwood. This chain had been filed to cut soft green pine and was too aggressive. Using chain that has been sharpened too aggressively can cause a number of problems: kickback, jumping, stick in curf and fatigue on the saw operator.

7 | Left side front angle shows using the roundness of the log for the beak

8 | Left rear view showing the wood removed from the rear of the neck to the top of the back and shoulder area.

9 Another view of the cuts to be made.

10 The wedge shape removed here may be accomplished in two ways. Three plunge cuts can be used, as was done here. Alternately, a series of cuts can be made from the bottom up to remove wood from this area.

11 Complete roughing out the rounded throat area. With a tapered carving bar, scribe in the curve as far as possible from both sides.

12 Make a series of cuts from the bottom up ending at your drawn line.

13 Now that you have a flat surface to draw on you can redraw marks better defining the head, neck and beak.

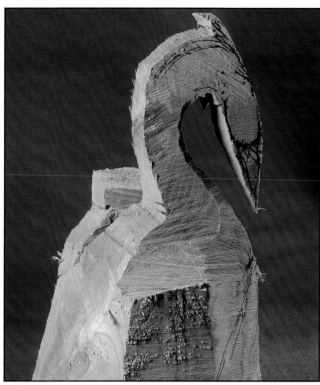

14 The shoulder on the opposite side of the carving has been formed down and over to the flora so that the future symmetry of the carving can be assured.

15 Remove the block of wood to expose the front of the chest, legs and flora and the water at the base. Make the angling down and inward cut. Then make a nearly precise plunge cut down the front side of the leg. Make the final horizontal cut to remove the block.

16 Shape and size the front view of the beak.

17 Shape and round the underside of the beak.

18 Skim the underside to reduce thickness.

19 Defining the crest from the head and neck.

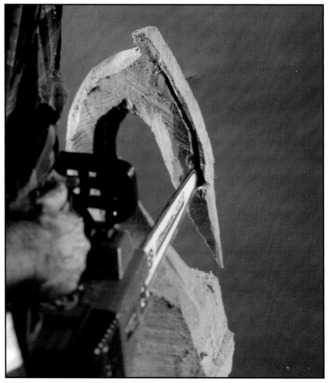

20 Make the beak, head, and eye definitions.

21 Round and reduce the head size with the upper trailing edge of the bar used in a downward motion.

22 Skim, smooth and shape the head, using the upper trailing edge of the bar again.

23 The chest and body can now be drawn out more closely in proportion to the head and neck. You may use a marker, the tip of your saw or your mind's eye to mark this area.

24 Leaving at least twice as much wood as necessary, mark the legs down to the water level .

25 Facing the carving from the front, use the center alignment of the beak to determine the spacing between the legs.

26 Start the center line plunge cut. Start the cut with the rear of the bar lower than the center of the tip to the perpendicular. After the tip is safely submerged in the wood, start cutting in and down. Be careful not to mar the area that will become the tail and lower portion of the body

27 Make two plunge cuts on the outer side of each leg parallel with the center cut.

28 The excess wood on the non-flora side of the carving may be removed with two in cuts to the outside of the leg.

29 | Better define the under-wing area.

30 | Make a plunge cut to begin forming the rear of the legs and flora.

31 | Being careful not to remove too much wood from the tail area.

32 | Two in cuts can be made from the rear to meet exactly with the top and bottom of the plunge cut.

33 Start to define the flora side wing from the flora.

34 Round and shape the chest and belly to meet with the front of the legs.

35 Flat horizontal plunge cuts remove some of the wood between the two legs.

36 Note the inside surface of the flora-side legs has been cut to its minimum. All future wood removed to thin the leg from this view should be on the side of the leg nearest the flora.

37 Now that I can better determine the balance and alignment of the body and legs, I am removing some of the excess thickness using front and rear plunge cuts.

38 Round, shape and thin to acquire the desired shape.

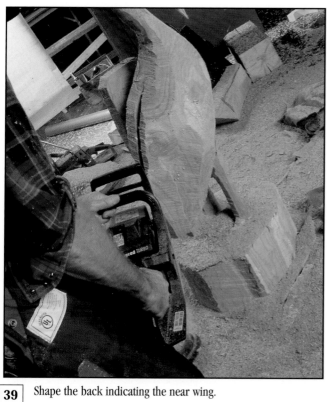

39 Shape the back indicating the near wing.

40 Define the far wing and tail.

41   Thin and shape the flora.

42   Separate the parts of the flora to give it character and depth.

43   When thinning and shaping flora, keep in mind that it must be thick enough to support the weight of the body of the bird and keep the stress off the thin legs

44   Near the end of the project, some of the thinning and shaping can be accomplished with texturing strokes.

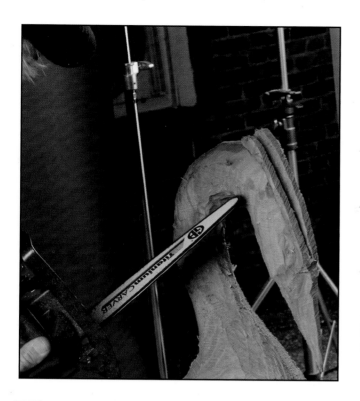

45 | Use texture strokes to finalize the shape of the area under the neck.

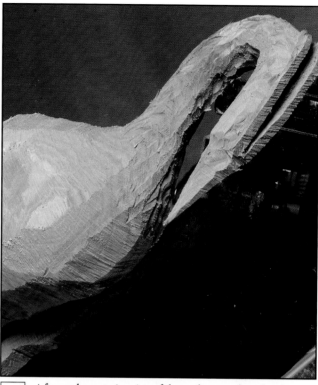

46 | A forward quartering view of the neck curve shaped with a fanning motion of the detailing bar.

47 | Roughly locate the knee joint.

48 | Draw in the lines to indicate rows of feathers.

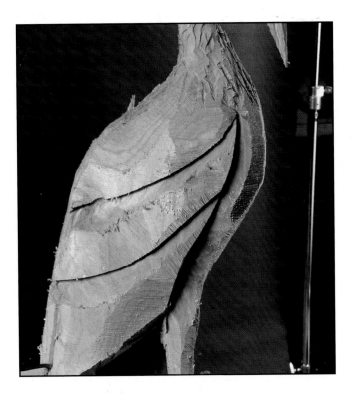

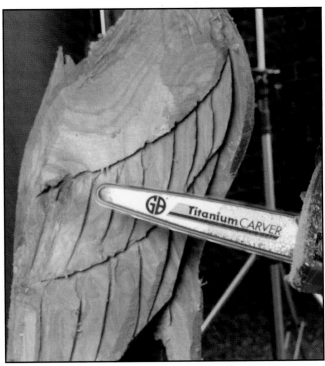

49 Separate the rows of feathers.

50 These bottom two rows of feathers were first drawn in the wood with a series of cuts perpendicular to the wood. Then the tapered rear edges were formed with the saw held as shown in photo.

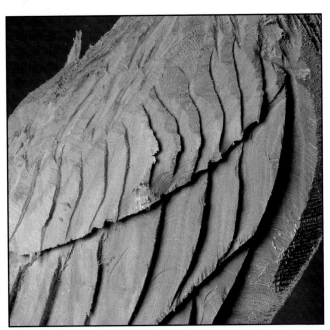

51 This top row of feathers was made by merely making a series of slightly angled cuts.

52 The smaller and softer neck features can be achieved by gently scribing them with the tip of the bar.

The finished and painted heron is ready for sale or display.

TOTEM POLES

Any project, and especially totem poles, should begin with a mental or written list of what you have and don't have. Tools, skill, design, material, transportation, time, space, financing, preservation and installation all come into play ten-fold when creating a totem pole.

Compared to six-, eight- and ten-foot carvings, totem poles of 24 feet or more require an incredible amount of logistical preparation: 1) find a tree of the desired species that contains a suitable 30-foot log; 2) move the log to a suitable area to be picked up and transported to the carving site; 3) prepare a portion to be buried underground after the totem is carved; 4) transport the pole to the set-up site (hopefully where someone else has already dug the hole); 5) unload the totem pole and attach wings and any other protruding features; 6) set the pole in the hole and back-fill around it, and 7) turn the pole in the direction your customer wants it facing before doing the final tamping and filling.

To design a totem pole, I use simplified designs that have been slightly modified from authentic Pacific Northwest totem poles. Research is important because of the nature of the totem pole. Pole carvings designed by those who have never seen a real totem pole or who choose to wander off on their own are not totem poles at all, but rather just a long pole of expensive, time-consuming carvings.

I draw all of the characters I commonly use on my totem poles on paper. Each character is in proportion to the others and all face the same direction. I copy and cut out the characters to aid me in designing a totem pole. This method also helps my customers to choose a custom design to their liking.

The Log

Geographic location and trees indigenous to the area are, of course, two major factors either extremely for or hard against procuring a suitable log for a totem pole project. If there is softwood logging in your area, you should be able to obtain a totem log from a local logger or sawmill with a minimum investment of time and money. If you live in an area where you have to procure your wood from an ornamental shade tree service, you will most likely have to do a lot more work to obtain a suitable log.

Several chain saw carvers, including myself, are both professional tree climbers and loggers who maintain the tools and skills to safely harvest logs for totem pole projects. If you do not have the skills or the equipment (experience notwithstanding), please do not attempt such work.

Currently I have a 150-acre wooded lot adjoining my carving field. I have marked potential totem trees with a "T" using a spray can. I cut only enough logs at a time for current needs, and then skid them to the field with a standard logging skidder. Very few carvers have such luxury.

Transportation and Installation

Currently I am using a standard northeastern logging truck with a Barko 80 self-contained loader for transporting and setting up most of the 30-foot totem poles I carve. For one delivery close to New York City, we used an 18-foot flatbed stake truck with a lift tailgate. The pole's traveling position was over the cab, supported and lashed to the front rack. The butt of the pole rested on top of the up-right power tailgate. We used several sets of cross braces on the bed for further support, stability and safety.

A local backhoe operator set up this pole. If a backhoe's reach or power is insufficient

A custom totem pole points the way to a customer's woodland home.

for the job, the operator will have to cut a ramp down into the hole and slide the pole over the ramp until the pole is near the opposite side of the hole, then insert an 8-foot plank upright in the hole across from the ramp. The pick can then be made above the center of balance. Guide ropes attached below the wings with a running bowline can assist the backhoe and increase safety. I use two men with peaveys or cant hooks to pivot the up-righted pole in exactly the correct direction before the hole is completely back-filled and tamped.

For those who live where log trucks are out of the question, tree services with loading cranes mounted on dump trucks are suitable for both transporting and setting up a 30-foot pole. Pole trailers, such as the ones you see your local electric and phone company construction crews use, can sometimes be rented at a heavy construction rental store. If you plan to carve and position more than one totem pole in your carving career, look for an inexpensive vehicle at an auction or auto salvage and sales yard.

In the Ground

One commonly asked question is how to prevent the underground portion of the pole from rotting. Most frequently, I insert a 14-foot section of old, heavily-creosoted electric or phone pole, or more modern pressure-treated pole, into a 7-foot long opening carved into the bottom rear of the totem pole. I often shave 7 feet of the utility pole on three sides to make it flat. This expedites the pattern-making process for the slot and assures a snugger fit. I use a standard chain saw to remove most of the wood from the slot. I then use a Log Wizard planer/router attachment on one of my chain saws to clean up

and smooth out the slot. I test-fit the utility pole in the back of the totem pole at the carving site, but I do not attach it until I reach the set-up site.

Once on-site, I unload the totem pole onto 10x10 skids to prevent soiling and marring of the pole. I insert the utility pole into the slot in the back of the totem and drill three 5/8 in. holes through the totem pole and the utility pole. As each hole is drilled, I drive a 3/8 in. threaded rod through the hole. I cut off the excess rod with a hacksaw, add the six nuts and washers, and bolt the two units securely together.

Before Raising

Any protruding parts need to be secured on the totem pole before it is raised. For me, these are most often wings. I use 10 in. or longer 3/8 in. lag bolts to attach the 3-in.-thick chain-saw-milled wings into 3 in. deep pre-cut notches in the back of the totem pole.

To prevent excess damage to the totem pole during raising we use nylon slings rather than chains or cables. We also attach at least one guide rope below the wings using a running bowline, in case any unforeseen problems arise. In cases where mechanical power and/or sufficient reach are limited, the ground hole can be trenched and the pole dragged in, lifted and braced gradually.

Some of the 30-foot totem poles I deliver are installed by contractors working under a landscape architect. They often use lots of concrete and steel—even metal strapping—around the pole. Such operations can cost more than the pole. My advice to those who want to make totem poles: Stay away from that kind of work and stick to carving. Be sure you make a

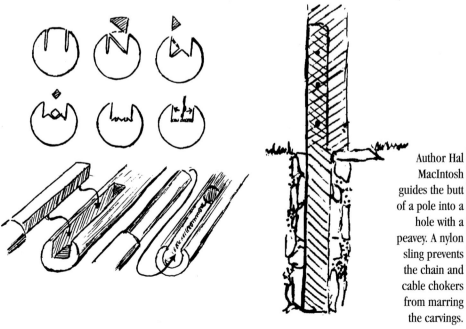

Author Hal MacIntosh guides the butt of a pole into a hole with a peavey. A nylon sling prevents the chain and cable chokers from marring the carvings.

Elevating the totem pole log will give you a more comfortable working height and ease the stress on your back, arms and legs. It will also make it easier to roll the log as you work all four sides.

detailed written and dated statement as to what exactly you will do for a given price.

Carving Tips

- Elevate the totem log on two cross logs or beams. This will make it easier to roll the log while you are peeling and carving it.
- If the log is bowed and if it is large enough, try to straighten the pole before carving it. If the log is too small to allow for excess wood removal, I prefer to position the bulge up. A slight bow will tend to disappear in the design.
- Many logs are oval or egg-shaped. Attempt to have the most symmetrical shape pointing up, perpendicular to your crossbeams. This is where you should carve your characters.
- If the log is dry, a snapped chalk line can be used to indicate the centerline. Lightly mark the line with your carving bar saw. If the log is wet, run a rope or baling twine down the log. Paint along the line for a visible marker.
- Mark the divisions on the log where each character will begin and end.

Wings and other elements that protrude from the main pole are carved separately and inserted on site. This pair of wings will be attached to a 2x8 placed in an 8-in.-wide notch in the back of the totem pole.

1 MILLION DESIGN IDEAS

Coming up with ideas for chain saw carvings doesn't have to be hard. Take a look at how easy it is to start with five subjects and end up with one million very different ideas.

Humans

1. Old Adult
2. Adult
3. Teen
4. Adolescent
5. Infant

• Each of the above as male and female, 5 x 2 = 10

• Each of the above in five different facial bone structures, 5 x 10 = 50

• Each of the above in the following:

1. thin
2. Near perfect
3. Heavy
4. Obese
5. Ridiculously fat

• Multiplying those 5 by the 50 above equals 250 ideas.

Now, let's take those 250 people and use them to represent various activities and dress over the past 3,000 years: dress military uniforms, combat military uniforms, warrior, chief, heavy labor attire, light labor attire, business attire, high fashion, sea outfits, mountain forest clothes, tropical clothes, just to mention a few.

Next, let's glance over sporting activities for the past 3000 years for males only. There are horse riding events, ball games, stick games, track and field events, ice events.... and many more. Not to mention all the different poses. We're already over one million.

Finally, take all those ideas and carve each of them as three-dimensional sculptures, relief carvings and pierced carvings. Now, we're way over one million. And notice I have not so far used any man-made tools or people making them or using them. I have not mentioned man-mad inventions for transportation on land, air or sea. Neither have I mentioned appliances or fixtures used by man, such as bathtubs, sinks or basins. Nor have I mentioned dwellings or types of architecture and furniture that can be employed into many a composition. I also have not mentioned Prehistoric man or wildlife, which in itself provides thousands of ideas for chainsaw carvings. Nor have I mentioned the thousands of state or province and country emblems and flags, nor those of countless organizations.

Dogs

• Man's selective mating of dogs has resulted in some 400 distinct breeds of standardized animals.

• Take 400 x 3 for male, female and pup and that adds up to 1200 designs.

• Now let's take only five types of mixed breeds multiplied by our 1200 purebred ideas. 1200 x 5 = 6000

• Add to that our original 1200 and you get 7200 in domestic dogs alone in a simple standing fashion.

• Finally, take that number and design each in these four poses: sitting on hind legs, laying down, running and jumping. Using only these four poses provides 28,800 design ideas.

If you were to mix the domestic dog ideas with most of the human design— as would likely occur in life—the figures would be quite substantial.

Wildlife

Take a look at a few composition ideas using hoofed mammals of North America.

1. Collared Peccary
2. European Wild Hog
3. Elk
4. Whitetailed Deer
5. Mule Deer
6. Moose
7. Caribou
8. Pronghorn
9. Bison
10. Big Horn Sheep
11. Dall's Sheep
12. Mountain Goat

• Multiply these 12 species by two for male and female. 12 x 2 = 24

• Add 12 for infants. 24 + 12 = 36

• Add 24 for immature animals of each sex. 36 + 24 = 60

Let's take a few common activities of everyday life.

1. Lying down
2. Standing into the wind
3. Feeding
4. Moving

• Multiply our 60 animals by these four activities. 4 x 60 = 240

• Take all of the above in conflict with five species of predators. 5 x 240 = 1200

• Two bulls fighting at two age levels for each of our original 12 gives us 24 more designs.

• Male with female for each of our original 12 gives us another 12. Mother with young gives us 12. Mother with immature gives us 12. 12 + 12 + 12 = 36

• Take jumping, leaps and bounds in three different fashions, such as front feet on the ground, hind feet on the ground and midway in the jump. Multiply these three movement ideas by our first 60. 3 x 60 = 180

• Now let's add up the ideas we have so far for hoofed mammals of North America. 180 + 1200 + 36 + 24 = 1440 is our total for three-dimensional compositions of the 12 species of animals.

Let's photograph the 1440 projects from six angles and do relief and pierced relief carvings from the photos. 6 x 1440 = 8640. That's 8,640 chainsaw carving composition ideas of North American hoofed mammals.

Let's move along to other North American wild animals.

1. Raccoon
2. Gray and Red Wolves
3. Gray Fox
4. Red Fox
5. Arctic Fox
6. Coyote
7. Jaguar
8. Mountain Lion
9. Lynx
10. Bob Cat
11. Harbor Seal
12. Walrus
13. Woodchuck
14. Yellow Bellied Marmot
15. Hoary Marmot
16. Gray Squirrel
17. Fox Squirrel
18. Tassel Eared Squirrel
19. Arctic Ground Squirrel
20. Prairie Dog
21. Porcupine
22. Brown Rat
23. Wood Rat
24. Cottontail Rabbit
25. Varying Hare
26. Arctic Hare
27. Jackrabbit
28. European Rabbit
29. Opossum
30. Mink
31. Skunks
32. Otter
33. Sea Otter
34. Pine Martin
35. Fisher
36. Weasels
37. Badgers
38. Wolverines
39. Beavers
40. Muskrats

Now using the 40 species let's do something similar to what we did with the hoofed mammals.

• Take one mature male of each 40 species, one immature male of each 40 species and one young of each 40 species. 3 x 40 = 120

• Now take one female of each 40 species alone, one female of each 40 species with two young and one female of each 40 species with four young. 3 x 40 = 120

• One male of each of the 40 species fighting another male of the same species. 40 design ideas

• One male of each of the 40 species fighting five different species of predators. 5 x 40 = 200

• Male and female of each species together. 40 design ideas

Add those all together and you have 520 design ideas. 120 + 120 + 40 + 200 + 40 = 520

Now take each of the 40 species in the five different compositions of the five actions below.

1. Feeding
2. Running
3. Sleeping
4. Swimming
5. Escaping

5 x 5 =25, 25 x 40 = 1000

Add up all the designs for North American wild animals, 1000 + 520, and you have 1520 design ideas.

Now let's photograph these 1520 projects from six angles and use the photos for pierced relief and relief carvings. 6 x 1520 gives you 9,120 ideas for realistic non-hoofed North American wild animals.

I have not mentioned tree dens or earthen or wood dens, which can be employed with all 40 of these animals. Nor have I mentioned their everyday social life with other animals, birds, fishes, reptiles and plant life around them. I have also not mentioned these animals in their relationships with an and his over 400 purebred dogs and 294,000 mixed breeds.

Repeat this exercise with other mammals on the other continents. In Africa alone, there are over 70 kinds of antelope, three kinds of giraffes, three kinds of zebras, plus elephants, rhino, big cats, and wild dogs. This accounts for over 80 species of good-sized African wildlife.

Now let's take the 8,640 ideas we had for North American hoofed mammals and divide it by 12 for the 12 species we included. $8640 \div 12 = 720$. Now let's use this number times our 80 aforementioned African species. $720 \times 80 = 57600$. That's 57, 600 compositions with a minimal number of African wildlife.

We have not yet accounted for any of the vast number of wildlife species that inhabit Australia, South America, Europe, Asia or the thousands of islands. Nor have we mentioned the thousands of species of reptiles, fish and plant life and the variety of insects around the world.

So let's add up the three numbers we have so far: 57,600 American wildlife, 8,640 North American hoofed mammals, 9, 120 other North American animals. $57600 + 8640 + 9120 = 75360$.

Now let's multiply this number times 20 for the remaining land and sea areas on the planet that are occupied by wildlife species. $75360 \times 20 = 1507200$. That's over a million and a half design for wild mammals, fish and reptiles. Now you can try each of these compositions in stylized and abstract. $2 \times 1507200 = 3104400$.

This final number excludes humans, birds, bears and domestic animals.

BEARS

Let's take the three shapes of North American bears: black, polar and grizzly (or Kodiak). If you had a half-hour video of a black bear in the wild with two cubs you could pick out over 100 interesting compositions of the group or each individual. That would be times three for the three main shapes, and that number times six for relief and pierced relief. That's 1,800 ideas just for realistic bears.

Let's multiply that number times three for adding bears of various styles, dressed bears, dancing bears, sport playing bears and cartoon bears doing all sorts of human activities and professions. That brings us up to 5,400 ideas with no accounting for 10-inch or 10-foot carvings.

CARVING HUMANS

Most artists for the past 3,000 years have proportioned humans by head length. Leonardo used a seven-heads scale. Vitruvious used a six-head scale. The Venus de Milo measures eight heads, as does the Farness Hercules.

My personal belief is that chain saw carvers should try to use 7½ to 8 heads. Many chain saw carvers are guilty of starting out a carving with the head too big and ending up with the legs too short or the body too narrow for the head. I have included the following proportion charts and notes for chainsaw carvers who wish to carve the human form. Please note that these measurements are for adults and that age will change the proportions. If you are going to carve nudes, please refer to a book on anatomy.

- The width of the shoulder is almost two heads.
- The midway distance in the 8-head scale is the crotch for adults.
- The hips are 1½ heads.
- The arm span is the same as the height.

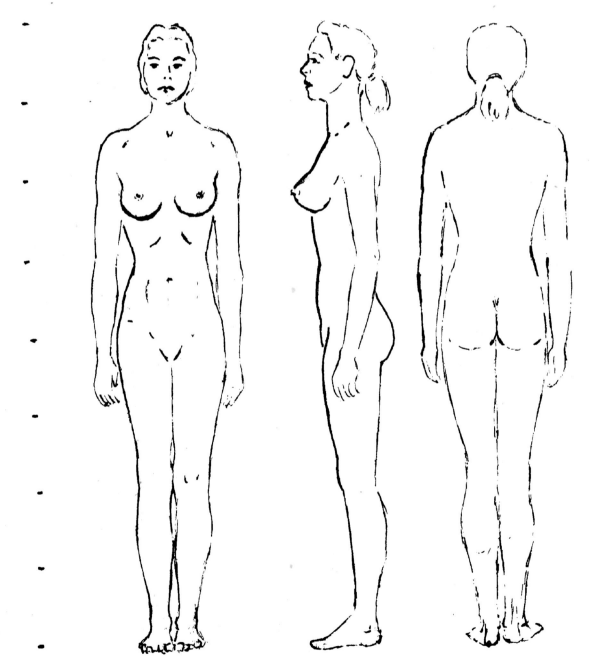

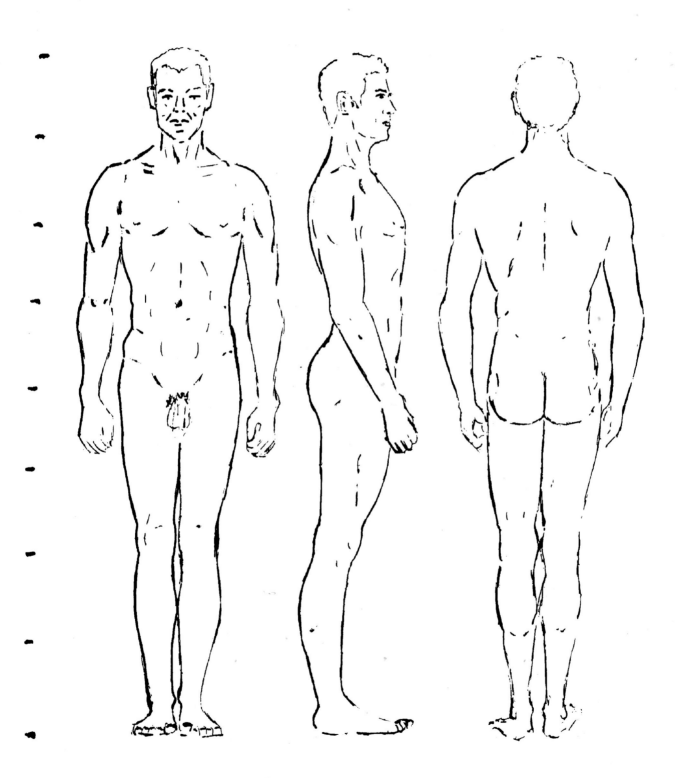

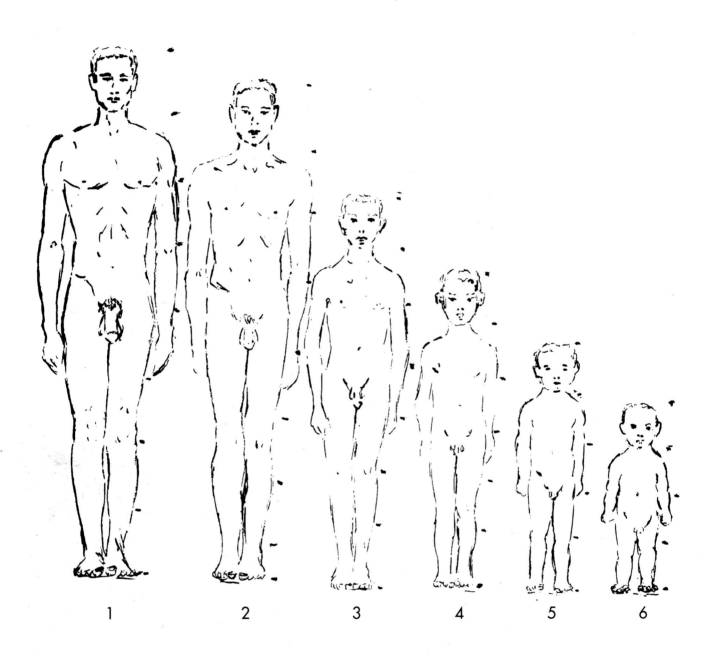

Approximate Proportions of Modern Man
According to age, using the 8-head method for adults

1	Six-foot adult	8 heads tall	each head 9 inches
2	15 year old	7.5 heads	each head 9 inches
3	10 year old	7 heads tall	each head 7.5 inches
4	5 year old	6 heads tall	each head 7 inches
5	3 year old	5 heads tall	each head 6.5 inches
6	1 year old	4 heads tall	each head 6 inches

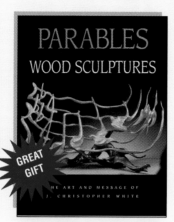

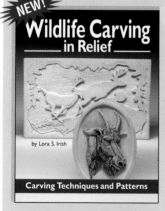

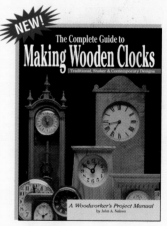

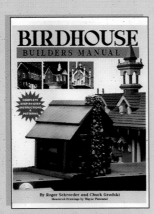
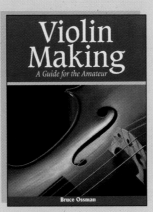
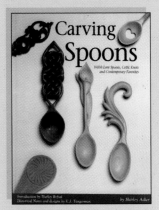
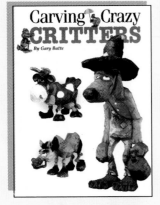

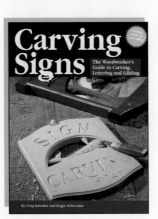
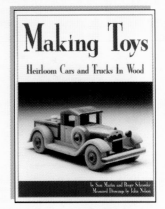

Carving Books From the Experts

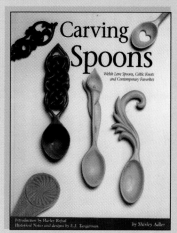

FOX# 092-2 $14.95
Carving Spoons
By Shirley Adler

Spoons are fun, simple projects to develop your carving creativity and express yourself.
• 23 full-size ready-to-use patterns
• Full color step-by-step instructions
• Features Welsh love spoons and Celtic knots

FOX# 104-X $14.95
Making Lawn Ornaments
in Wood
By Paul Meisel

Stop traffic with these popular lawn & garden accessories.
• Complete instructions & patterns for 34 projects
• Full color gallery
• "How-to-paint" mixing chart

MARY DUKE GULDAN

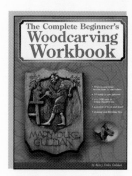

FOX# 085-X $9.95
Complete Beginner's
Woodcarving
Workbook

Simply the best, easiest guide to carving ever! All you need is a knife and several simple gouges to get started.
• 10 projects
• Complete patterns and instructions

FOX# 033-7 $14.95
Woodcarver's
Workbook—
Carving Animals

A great beginner's book on carving. Learn carving basics, safety tips and how to get the most out of your patterns.
• 8 full-size patterns
• Step-by-step instructions

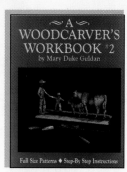

FOX# 037-X $14.95
Woodcarver's
Workbook #2

A continuation in the author's beginner's line of carving books. More great projects to improve your carving skills.
• Ready-to-use patterns
• Solid carving tips and techniques

BEST SELLERS

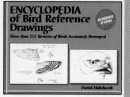

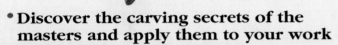